URBAN TRAILS

MADISON

Downtown · UW Campus
Dane County · Ice Age Trail

ANDREA DEBBINK

MOUNTAINEERS BOOKS

MOUNTAINEERS BOOKS is dedicated to the exploration, preservation, and enjoyment of outdoor and wilderness areas.

1001 SW Klickitat Way, Suite 201, Seattle, WA 98134
800-553-4453, www.mountaineersbooks.org

Printed in China
First edition, 2025

Design: Jen Grable
Layout: Ellis Failor-Rich
Cartographer: Bart Wright, Lohnes+Wright
All photographs are by the author unless otherwise indicated.
Cover photograph: *The oak savanna in Prairie Moraine County Park (Trail 29)*
Frontispiece: *Fall colors in Badger Prairie County Park (Trail 25)*

Library of Congress Cataloging-in-Publication data is on file for this title at https://lccn.loc.gov/2024049530

Mountaineers Books titles may be purchased for corporate, educational, or other promotional sales, and our authors are available for a wide range of events. For information on special discounts or booking an author, contact our customer service at 800-553-4453 or mbooks@mountaineersbooks.org.

Printed on FSC®-certified materials.

ISBN (paperback):978-1-68051-727-9
ISBN (ebook): 978-1-68051-728-6

MIX
Paper | Supporting responsible forestry
FSC® C188448
www.fsc.org

An independent nonprofit publisher since 1960

CONTENTS

SOUTHWEST

NORTHWEST

Greene Prairie at the UW Arboretum's Grady Tract (Trail 4)

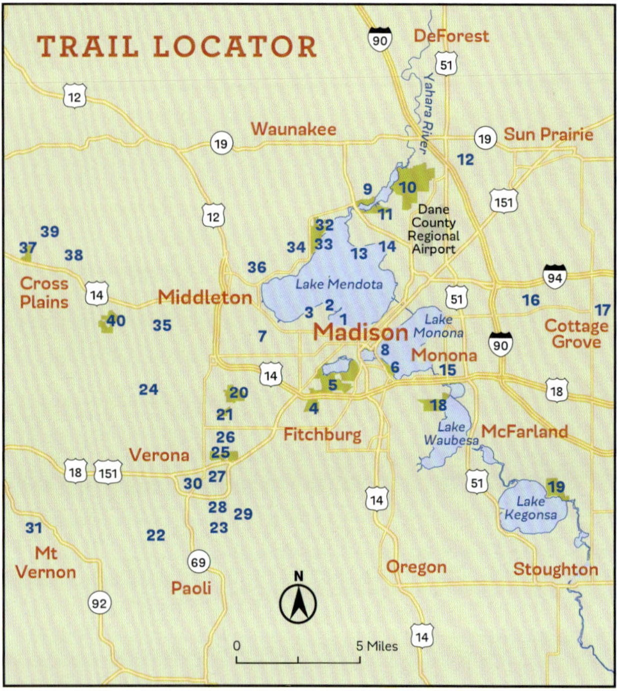
TRAIL LOCATOR
DeForest
Yahara River
Waunakee
Sun Prairie
Dane County Regional Airport
Lake Mendota
Cross Plains
Middleton
Madison
Lake Monona
Monona
Cottage Grove
Fitchburg
Lake Waubesa
McFarland
Verona
Lake Kegonsa
Mt Vernon
Paoli
Oregon
Stoughton
N
0
5 Miles

TRAILS AT A GLANCE

Trail and/or Park	Distance	Walk	Hike	Run	Kids	Dogs
CENTRAL						
1. Lakeshore Nature Preserve: Howard Temin Path	4.2 miles	•	•	•	•	•
2. Lakeshore Nature Preserve: Picnic Point	3.6 miles	•	•	•	•	•
3. Lakeshore Nature Preserve: Eagle Heights Woods	1.3 miles	•	•		•	•
4. UW Arboretum: Grady Tract	3.7 miles	•	•	•	•	
5. UW Arboretum: Central Loop	2.4 miles	•	•	•	•	
6. Turville Point Conservation Park	1.8 miles	•	•	•	•	
7. Owen Conservation Park	1.4 miles	•	•		•	
8. Monona Lake Loop: Olin Park	4.2 miles	•		•	•	•
NORTHEAST						
9. Cherokee Marsh Natural Resource Area	3.8 miles	•	•		•	•
10. Cherokee Marsh Conservation Park: North	3 miles		•		•	
11. Cherokee Marsh Conservation Park: South	1.2 miles	•	•	•	•	
12. Token Creek County Park	3.3 miles	•	•	•	•	•
13. Governor's Island	1 mile	•			•	•
14. Warner Park	1.5 miles	•		•	•	•

Trail and/or Park	Distance	Walk	Hike	Run	Kids	Dogs
SOUTHEAST						
15. Aldo Leopold Nature Center	1 mile	•	•		•	
16. Door Creek Park	2.1 miles	•	•	•	•	•
17. Glacial Drumlin State Trail	5.6 miles	•	•	•	•	•
18. Capital Springs State Recreation Area	3.4 miles	•	•		•	•
19. Lake Kegonsa State Park	2.7 miles	•	•	•	•	
SOUTHWEST						
20. Elver Park	3.1 miles	•	•	•	•	partial
21. Ice Age Trail: Madison Segment	3.2 miles one way	•	•	•	•	•
22. Madison School Forest	3.9 miles		•		•	partial
23. Scheidegger Forest	1.1 miles	•	•	•	•	
24. Valley View Preserve	3.8 miles	•	•		•	•
25. Badger Prairie County Park	2.3 miles	•	•	•	•	•
26. Ice Age Trail: Verona Segment North	3.7 miles	•	•	•	•	•
27. Ice Age Trail: Verona Segment Central	3.6 miles	•	•	•	•	•
28. Ice Age Trail: Verona Segment South	1.6 miles	•	•		•	•
29. Prairie Moraine County Park	3 miles		•		•	•
30. Military Ridge State Trail: Verona	5 miles	•	•	•	•	•
31. Donald County Park	5.2 miles		•	•	•	•
NORTHWEST						
32. Governor Nelson State Park: Morningside Trail	2.4 miles	•	•	•	•	•
33. Governor Nelson State Park: Woodland Trail	1.6 miles	•	•	•	•	•
34. Holy Wisdom Monastery	2.3 miles	•	•	•	•	
35. Pope Farm Conservancy	1.7 miles	•	•	•	•	

Trail and/or Park	Distance	Walk	Hike	Run	Kids	Dogs
36. Pheasant Branch Conservancy	4.2 miles	•	•	•	•	•
37. Festge County Park	3.5 miles	•	•	•	•	•
38. Ice Age Trail: Cross Plains Segment	3.1 miles		•		•	•
39. Ice Age Trail: Table Bluff Segment	4.4 miles		•		•	•
40. Cross Plains State Park	3 miles		•		•	•

Tree canopy in Eagle Heights Woods (Trail 3)

INTRODUCTION

TRAILS FOR FUN AND FITNESS IN YOUR BIG BACKYARD

IF YOU ASK A MADISON LOCAL where to hike, they'll probably name one of southern Wisconsin's scenic state parks like Devil's Lake, or a popular state natural area like Parfrey's Glen. These destinations, and others like them, are beautiful places with easy-to-navigate trails and dramatic scenery. But head there on a summer Saturday—or *any* weekend with good weather—and you'll likely find parking lot traffic jams and endless streams of people and pets. A hike in one of these places can often feel more like a trip to Disney World and less like a nature retreat.

Until I wrote this guidebook, I assumed that most local trails were like this too. After all, the Madison metro area is home to more than half a million people. But I was in for a surprise. I spent a year hiking the forty routes in this book, mostly on weekends in spring, summer, or fall. Yet I saw few people, even on trails that were surrounded by city neighborhoods. From this, it'd be natural to conclude that people aren't interested in nature or hiking, but the data doesn't support it. According to the most recent Outdoor Participation Trends Report from the Outdoor Industry Association, hiking is the most popular outdoor activity in the US—and its popularity is growing. In a similar survey conducted by the Wisconsin Department of Natural Resources, 68 percent of Wisconsin residents go hiking each year. Plus, what about the overflowing parking lots at the better-known trails?

Instead, I think many of us in Madison simply don't know about all the incredible hiking opportunities our community offers. I'm a seasoned hiker and I've lived here for more than twenty years. Yet as I wrote this book, I came across trails that were brand-new to me—one only a couple of miles from where I live. In my research, I realized that I had gotten used to hiking in a few familiar haunts and had stopped venturing beyond them. But as I learned—and you will too—Madison is full of opportunities for outdoor adventure hiding in plain sight.

The purpose of this guide is to introduce you to some of the many hiking trails that weave around and through the Madison area—and a bit beyond. Lakes are at the heart of the city, but our home here is also defined by woodlands, moraines, oak savannas, prairies, wetlands, ponds, rivers, and creeks. The trails in the following pages will lead you through all these habitats and more. Along the way, you'll not only get fresh air, exercise, and a bit of adventure, but you'll learn the story of the land around us—the story of long-ago glaciers, the Ho-Chunk people and their ancestors before them, farming and agriculture, weather, climate change, and the newer story of ecological restoration. It's a story that's still being written—and now you're a part of it too.

Exploring the forest at Cherokee Marsh Conservation Park: North (Trail 10)

HOW TO USE THIS GUIDE

THIS EASY-TO-USE GUIDE PROVIDES INFORMATION about hiking routes in Madison and the surrounding area, including quick facts, maps, and route descriptions. Whether you're looking for a lakeside stroll in the heart of downtown, a half-day adventure in the Driftless, or a kid-friendly walk in a wildflower meadow, you'll find all of these and more in this book. To ensure accuracy and up-to-date information, I've traveled these routes myself. That said, routes and conditions do change, so check the status of a trail or park before you go, using the contact information provided in the book's Resources section.

THE ROUTES

This book includes forty routes and trail systems in and around the greater Madison area, including destinations in Middleton, Cross Plains, Waunakee, Monona, Stoughton, and beyond. Paved routes are typically designated as "paths," and unpaved routes as "trails." Each route begins with the park or trail name, followed by a block of information that details the following:

DISTANCE. This is the roundtrip mileage (unless otherwise noted) of the featured route, which I measured with GPS and/or mapping software. Mileage is not always consistent across maps, guidebooks, or GPS trackers, but the distances provided here should be within a few tenths of a mile. Total mileage of trails within a park, preserve, or natural area are noted in the route description when applicable.

A bench overlooks Lost Lake at Holy Wisdom Monastery. (Trail 34)

ELEVATION GAIN. Elevation gain is the cumulative difference of vertical change on a trail. This is not only the difference between the route's highest and lowest points, but for all other significant changes in elevation along the way.

HIGH POINT. This is the trail's highest elevation.

DIFFICULTY. The length and elevation gain of a trail, and its type of surface, determine its difficulty. In this book, most trails range from easy to moderate for the average walker, hiker, or runner, but difficulty also depends on your fitness level and experience.

FITNESS. This category notes if the trail is best for walkers, hikers, or runners. Walkers and runners may prefer paved trails, while hikers might choose rough or hilly ones—but users can walk, run, or hike any of them (unless it's not allowed).

FAMILY-FRIENDLY. Check this category to see if a trail is suitable for children. Things to watch out for, like steep trails or vehicle or bike traffic, are listed here.

DOG-FRIENDLY. Here you'll find whether or not dogs are allowed on the trail, and if any rules or permits apply.

AMENITIES. A park's features might include restrooms, drinking water, picnic tables, shelters, benches, interpretive signs, learning centers, campgrounds, and so on. **Note:** The availability, condition, or service of trailhead restrooms can vary dramatically. Restrooms can be as basic as vault toilets or portable outhouses, or as nice as flush toilets with hand-washing sinks. Some flush facilities might be closed in winter, with portable outhouses provided instead, but not always.

CONTACT/MAP. The organization or administrative body that manages the trail or park is listed here and is often the best source for current maps and trail conditions. All websites and phone numbers for these organizations are in the Resources section.

GPS. GPS coordinates are given for the featured route's trailhead. The format is listed in degrees and decimal minutes based on the WGS84 datum.

Approaching Frederick's Hill at Pheasant Branch Conservancy (Trail 36)

BEFORE YOU GO. Look here to find information about fees or permits and any other special considerations for the featured route.

GETTING THERE. Public Transit: If Madison Metro public buses go near the trailhead, this section identifies the route and stop locations, along with walking directions to the trailhead. **Driving:** This gives directions to the trailhead from the nearest highway, road, or neighborhood, as well as parking information.

Each trail description starts with a summary of the featured area, including its setting and natural and cultural history.

GET MOVING: The featured route is described in this section; it may also include additional highlights such as flora and fauna and points of historical, natural, or cultural interest.

GO FARTHER OR MAKE IT SHORTER: This section gives suggestions for extending or shortening the featured route.

PERMITS, REGULATIONS, AND PARK FEES

City and county parks departments oversee most of the trails and parks in this book. All but a few are free and do not require permits or fees. Destinations managed by the Wisconsin Department of Natural Resources, such as state parks, may require a vehicle permit or day-use fee. Each hike in this guide clearly states if a fee is charged or a pass is required. Regulations such as restricted hours and closures for certain occasions are indicated in each trail's information block.

ROAD AND TRAIL CONDITIONS

Although trails tend to stay mostly the same from year to year, conditions can change—sometimes quickly. Trails can flood, bridges can be washed out, and wind and storms

Black walnuts scatter across a trail in Cherokee Marsh Natural Resource Area (Trail 9)

can topple trees, in addition to ongoing natural processes like erosion. In the spring and after a significant weather event, it's wise to check trail and road conditions at your destination before heading out. It's also worth noting that trails don't take care of themselves. Nearly all the trails in this book were created and are actively managed by groups of volunteers, such as the Ice Age Trail Alliance or one of the many Friends Groups that support Wisconsin state parks. Consider joining a trail or conservation group in your area to help support local trails, or volunteer on one of their work days. You'll find a list of these organizations in the Resources section.

OUTDOOR ETHICS

The hikes in this book are on public lands that are managed by various organizations, and most have rules or regulations that visitors are expected to follow. (For instance, some public lands allow leashed dogs, while others don't allow dogs at all.) Wherever you go, it's important to know the property's rules so you don't harm the environment or hinder the experiences of other trail users. Even when there aren't specific rules to follow, keep certain principles in mind when participating in outdoor recreation. These are collectively known as "outdoor ethics" and help minimize our negative impact on the natural world. The Leave No Trace Center for Outdoor Ethics is an educational nonprofit founded to promote responsible enjoyment and active stewardship of the outdoors; it's a great resource. The organization is known for its seven principles that can be applied by anyone, whether you're backpacking in the wilderness or picnicking at a city park. They're helpful for hikers too.

- **Plan ahead and prepare.** For hikers, this can mean knowing your route and trail conditions ahead of time so you don't veer off-trail (either intentionally or by accident) and cause damage to plants and habitats; it can also help you stay safe.

- **Travel and camp on durable surfaces.** Always use established trails. Trampling can cause great harm to vegetation and other organisms.
- **Dispose of waste properly.** Some parks have trash and recycling collection on-site, while many trailheads don't. If public trash and recycling receptacles are not available, bring your trash or recyclables home with you. In outdoor lingo, this is known as "pack in, pack out." Also, always use park restroom facilities, or go before you arrive.
- **Leave what you find.** Some parks allow foraging of certain plants, such as wild raspberries, but many public lands prohibit collecting items from nature, such as plants, rocks, historical artifacts, and other items. Some things, such as bird feathers, eggs, and nests, are protected by federal law and should never be collected. In most cases, it's best to leave items in nature.
- **Minimize campfire impacts.** Some destinations in this book have fire rings that visitors can use. Only build campfires in designated rings in areas where fires are permitted. Never cut trees or plants for firewood.
- **Respect wildlife.** Always observe wild animals from a distance and never feed them. If you find an injured wild animal, call the Dane County Humane Society's Wildlife Center. They can assess the situation and let you know what to do.
- **Be considerate of others.** Remember that public lands are for all of us, and do your part to make the outdoors a welcoming place for others. For specifics, read the section on trail etiquette.

Summer at Pheasant Branch Conservancy (Trail 36)

ACCESSIBILITY

Everyone benefits from being in nature and out on a trail, but it's not always easy. If you're a hiker who uses a wheelchair or other mobility device, it can be difficult to determine if a trail is accessible for you, considering things like trailhead amenities, trail length and width, surface type, grade, and the presence of obstacles. With these in mind, there are several routes in this guide to consider:

- **Lakeshore Nature Preserve: Howard Temin Path** (Trail 1)
- **Lakeshore Nature Preserve: Picnic Point,** specifically the first segment (Trail 2)
- **Monona Lake Loop: Olin Park** (Trail 8)
- **Glacial Drumlin State Trail** (Trail 17)
- **Lake Kegonsa State Park,** specifically the Prairie Trail segment (Trail 19)
- **Military Ridge State Trail: Verona** (Trail 30)

In addition to the above, the following parks have trails and paths that may be accessible, depending on individual needs:

- **Capital Springs State Recreation Area (Madison):** The trailhead at Lake Farm County Park provides access to the paved 2.5-mile Lower Yahara River Trail and hiking trails. Across Lake Farm Road, you'll find the paved Capital City Trail.
- **Warner Park (Madison):** A 0.7-mile paved trail travels around this city park's lagoon and connects to turf and dirt hiking paths.
- **Salmo Pond County Park (Cross Plains):** A 0.4-mile level path circles this pond, which also offers three accessible fishing piers and two accessible shore fishing stations.
- **Jenni & Kyle Preserve (Fitchburg):** This county park was designed for people with disabilities, especially children. Amenities include accessible fishing, trails, picnic areas, and wheelchair swings.

An additional option to explore is renting an all-terrain wheelchair or other adaptive equipment from Access Ability Wisconsin. This nonprofit works to provide access to outdoor recreation for people with disabilities through adaptive equipment rental and community programs. For equipment reservations and locations in Dane County, contact Access Ability Wisconsin (see Resources).

The "rails-to-trails" accessible Military Ridge State Trail (Trail 30)

TRAIL ETIQUETTE

When you're hiking a trail, it's important to not only respect your surroundings but to respect fellow trail users, including other hikers, mountain bikers or cyclists, and equestrians. Here are some simple ways to show courtesy to other trail users and to the people who maintain the trails.

- **Observe the right-of-way.** In most cases, hikers, walkers, and runners should yield to other trail users because it's easier to move aside on foot. If you meet bicyclists, in-line skaters, or wheelchair users on a trail, move to let them pass. If you encounter horseback riders, step aside but stay in the horse's sight and say hello to make your presence known.
- **Stay on marked trails.** Don't take shortcuts or cut switchbacks or make new trails. This creates erosion, damages trails, and makes for costly trail repairs. It can also confuse other trail users and lead them astray.
- **Follow the rules of the park or trail.** Some trails are closed to certain types of users, including dogs and mountain bikes. In winter, some hiking trails are groomed for cross-country skiing and are closed to hiking. Even if a ski trail is open to hikers, yield to skiers and never walk on the groomed portions of the trail.
- **Keep dogs under control and clean up after them.** Most trails in this book that allow dogs require them to be leashed, and some destinations (like Dane County parks) require a dog permit. As a responsible dog owner, pack out your dog's waste bags, and don't leave them trailside to be collected (or forgotten) later; this is harmful to the environment and an eyesore for other trail users.
- **Mind the music.** If you like listening to music while you hike, wear earbuds and respect other trail users' right to peace and quiet.

WHAT TO BRING

For hikes of any length, including short ones, be sure to pack the Ten Essentials, a list of items developed by The Mountaineers that are important to have on hand in an emergency. The point of the Ten Essentials has always been to answer two basic questions: Can you prevent emergencies and respond positively should one occur? And can you safely spend a night—or more—outside? Use this list as a guide and tailor it to the needs of your outing.

1. **Navigation.** The fundamentals for navigation are a map (download or pick up a map of the area you plan to visit) or GPS device (like a cell phone with a GPS app). If you have these and know how to use them, also bring a compass, altimeter, and personal locator beacon.
2. **Headlamp.** If your hike runs late and you're caught out after dark, it'll be helpful to have a headlamp or flashlight to find your way back to the trailhead. Bring spare batteries too.
3. **Sun protection.** Even on rainy days, bring along sunscreen and sunglasses. Like many places, Wisconsin is known for its changeable weather, so it's smart to be prepared for all conditions.
4. **First-aid supplies.** Carry a small kit that contains bandages, gauze, blister treatment supplies, tweezers, pain reliever, and antibiotic ointment. If you have allergies (e.g., pollen or bees), you may want to bring allergy medication or an EpiPen.
5. **Knife.** In addition to a knife, a multitool can come in handy, as can basic repair items such as nylon cord, safety pins, and duct tape.
6. **Fire-making supplies.** Being forced to spend the night outside is not likely on these trails, but a campfire could provide welcome warmth in an emergency, so take along matches kept dry in a waterproof container.

A NOTE ABOUT SAFETY

Safety is an important concern in all outdoor activities. No guidebook can alert you to every hazard or anticipate the limitations of every reader. Therefore, the descriptions of roads, trails, routes, and natural features in this book are not representations that a particular place or excursion will be safe for your party. When you follow any of the routes described in this book, you assume responsibility for your own safety.

Under normal conditions, such excursions require the usual attention to traffic, road and trail conditions, weather, terrain, the capabilities of your party, and other factors. Keeping informed on current conditions and exercising common sense are the keys to a safe, enjoyable outing.

—Mountaineers Books

7. **Emergency shelter.** A rain poncho or garbage bag can serve as an emergency tarp. There are also lightweight tarps and bivvy sacks that can double as picnic blankets.
8. **Extra food.** Pack trail mix or protein bars for emergency pick-me-ups. For longer outings, carry a little extra.
9. **Extra water.** Bring enough water to stay hydrated for the length of the trail you visit. If the trailhead doesn't have drinking water, keep extra in your vehicle so you'll have some at the end of your hike too.
10. **Extra clothes.** Weather and temperature can change quickly, so it's always advisable to carry an extra insulating layer (e.g., fleece or sweater) and raingear.

HUNTING

Some destinations in this book are open to hunting. Season dates vary depending on the year and animal, so it's important to research this information for your specific hike before you go. In Wisconsin, deer and waterfowl hunting are the most common, and the seasons can range from September through January. If you use trails in areas open to hunters, make yourself visible by wearing blaze orange. If hiking with your dog, keep it leashed and dress it in blaze orange too.

Next page: A lakeside trail runs from Raymer's Cove to Eagle Heights Woods. (Trail 3)

CENTRAL

Downtown Madison—home to the University of Wisconsin, lively neighborhoods, a celebrated dining scene, and a slate of public events—may seem like an unlikely place for a hike. Yet some of the city's most scenic trails are found here as they meander along the lakefront (Monona, Mendota, or Wingra—you pick), cruise through campus, or follow hidden routes through restored woodlands and prairies just beyond the buzz of traffic.

Two of the city's most popular outdoor destinations lie in central Madison: the Lakeshore Nature Preserve (home to Picnic Point) and the UW–Madison Arboretum. Both places have miles of hiking trails and are easily accessible via public transportation for students and downtown residents. On the opposite side of the isthmus, the Monona Lake Loop and trails at Turville Point also offer calming doses of nature within sight of downtown.

1 Lakeshore Nature Preserve: Howard Temin Path

DISTANCE:	4.2 miles
ELEVATION GAIN:	70 feet
HIGH POINT:	870 feet
DIFFICULTY:	Easy
FITNESS:	Walkers, hikers, runners
FAMILY FRIENDLY:	Yes, but there can be a lot of bike and pedestrian traffic during the school year and on weekends.
DOG FRIENDLY:	Leashed dogs only
AMENITIES:	Parking ramp, restrooms, concessions, and dining options at Memorial Union. Public parking in Lot 130 at the west end of the Howard Temin Path.
CONTACT/MAP:	Lakeshore Nature Preserve (UW–Madison); map available online and on-site
GPS:	N 43°4'36.9"W 89°24'2.2"
BEFORE YOU GO:	Public parking is available in the Helen C. White parking ramp near the trailhead for an hourly fee, and in Lot 130 at the route's western end.

GETTING THERE

Public Transit: Madison Metro Route 80 stops in front of Memorial Union, and Routes D and B have stops within walking distance.

Driving: From University Avenue in downtown Madison, head north on North Park Street for 0.25 miles until it ends in a cul-de-sac. (The Helen C. White parking ramp is on the left.) This hike begins at the north side of the cul-de-sac.

For many university students, the Howard Temin Path is their first introduction to Madison's hiking trails. Yet like me, they may not even realize it. When I was a UW undergrad living in a lakeshore dorm, the Howard Temin Path, running nearly two miles from Memorial Union to Picnic Point, was merely

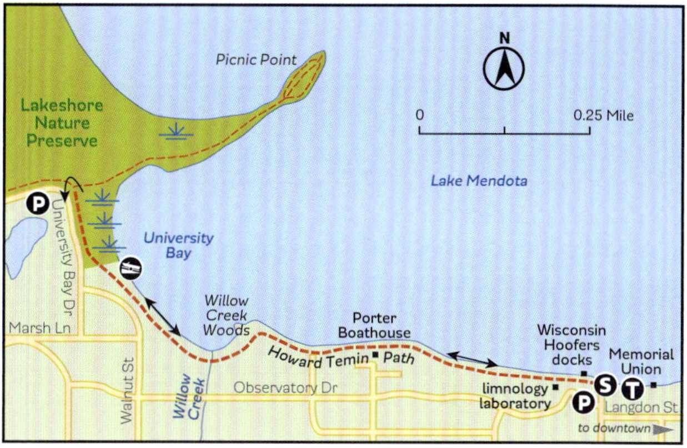

the scenic route to class and crew practice, not to mention, my usual running route. But together with the 2-mile Lake Mendota Path that loops around the tip of Picnic Point, the Howard Temin Path makes up one of Madison's most popular walking routes and hiking trails—officially known as the Lakeshore Path. It's not only a beautiful place to walk, it's an important link (for people and wildlife) between campus and the heart of the Lakeshore Nature Preserve.

GET MOVING

The Howard Temin Path begins just west of Memorial Union Terrace. Starting at the cul-de-sac on North Park Street, follow the sidewalk along the access road that heads west behind Helen C. White Hall. At the bottom of the hill, you can either begin walking on the paved path along Lake Mendota or continue to the end of the access road. Either way, after passing the docks for Wisconsin Hoofers, the university's outdoors club, keep right (lakeside) around UW's limnology laboratory. From here, you'll see a crushed-stone path ahead of you as it travels along the forested lakefront. Pedestrians and cyclists share this section of the route, so be aware of other trail users and stay to the right.

Catch a post-hike sunset at Memorial Union Terrace, a popular Madison gathering place.

This strip of land along the lake is technically part of the Lakeshore Nature Preserve, although the main preserve encompasses Picnic Point and adjacent land further ahead. There are a few benches along this section where you can sit by the lake to watch sailboats or wandering flocks of mallards. For the next half mile or so, the path follows the shoreline past several university residence halls, with stairs and connector paths leading to their grounds. At 0.6 mile, the path passes between the lake and the Porter Boathouse, home to the university's rowing teams. If boats are being loaded or unloaded, you may have to wait or detour around the south side of the building.

When you reach a small point at the 1-mile mark, you can take a more rugged detour through Willow Creek Woods on a side trail that parallels the Howard Temin Path. (This side trail rejoins the main path after a couple hundred yards.) Just beyond this point, the trail splits into two parallel paths, one for each direction. Follow the right path (nearest the lake) as you continue heading west. Next the path passes a small marsh where you may see and hear red-winged blackbirds, depending on the season, followed by a small boat launch and dock. The water to your right is known as University Bay, a natural harbor that continues to the end of Picnic Point.

As you near the turnaround point, you'll see a large marsh on the right and the narrow peninsula known as Picnic Point beyond that. The entrance to Picnic Point, at 1.7 miles, is the turnaround point for this hike. (The Howard Temin Path continues for another half mile along University Bay Drive to Oxford Road if you want to hike the entire path.) Follow the route in reverse—staying right when the path splits into two—to return to your starting point at the Memorial Union.

GO FARTHER

Rather than turning around at the Picnic Point entrance, continue hiking to the end of the point, then retrace your steps. This out-and-back will add another 1.6 miles to the total distance. Or combine this route and the 3.6-mile loop described in Trail 2 for a 7.8-mile outing.

2 Lakeshore Nature Preserve: Picnic Point

DISTANCE: 3.6 miles
ELEVATION GAIN: 180 feet
HIGH POINT: 920 feet
DIFFICULTY: Easy
FITNESS: Walkers, hikers, runners
FAMILY FRIENDLY: Yes
DOG FRIENDLY: Leashed dogs only
AMENITIES: Parking lot, interpretative info, benches, firepits, restrooms (en route)
CONTACT/MAP: Lakeshore Nature Preserve (UW–Madison); map available online and on-site
GPS: N 43°5'4.1" W 89°25'43.1"
BEFORE YOU GO: A new visitor center is scheduled to open at the Lakeshore Nature Preserve in 2026.

GETTING THERE

Public Transit: Madison Metro Route 80 stops at the Picnic Point entrance gate.

Driving: From University Avenue/Campus Drive, turn north onto University Bay Drive. Follow University Bay Drive for 1 mile, then turn right at Lot 130 to park. Parking is free on evenings and weekends; daytime visitors on weekdays must pay at the on-site pay station. The trailhead and entrance to Picnic Point is just north of the parking lot. Parking lots at Frautschi Point (2662 Lake Mendota Drive) and Raymer's

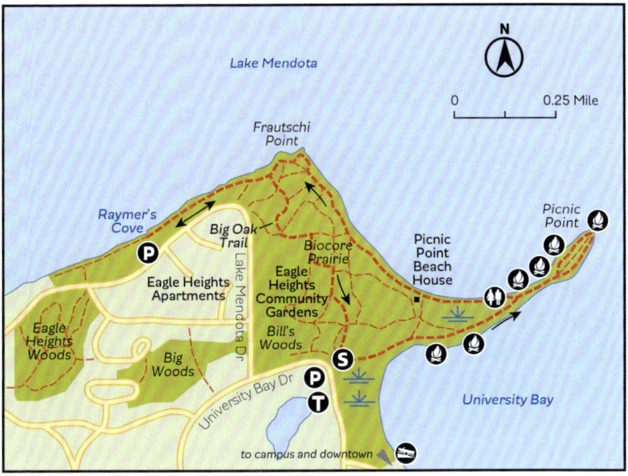

Cove (2900 Lake Mendota Drive) also offer free parking for Lakeshore Nature Preserve visitors.

When I was a student at the University of Wisconsin–Madison, my lakeside running route never took me beyond Picnic Point, the narrow peninsula that curves into Lake Mendota. Back then, I didn't realize this popular Madison destination and its well-trod path was only a small part of the much larger Lakeshore Nature Preserve. Now I know better. Any first-time hike through the Preserve *should* include a trek to the tip of Picnic Point, with its panoramic views of campus and the Wisconsin state capitol dome, but don't stop there. For an easy hike that explores the woods and prairie of this 300-acre gem, try this 3.6-mile lakeside loop that takes you on trails less traveled.

GET MOVING

The Lakeshore Nature Preserve's main entrance—at the western end of Picnic Point—is marked by an information kiosk and gate. In 2026, a visitor center is scheduled to open on this site. (From this point on, the trail is open to pedestrians only. Bikes must be left at the bike racks.) The crushed stone trail is flat and level as it takes a direct route to the tip of the point; keep right at all trail junctions to stay on route. This first mile is the busiest section of the hike, particularly on weekends when students, out-of-town visitors, and locals converge here. As you hike through the heart of the point, you'll pass plenty of places to stop for picnics, Madison skyline photo ops, and bird-watching. There are even six "fire circles" (firepits with cooking grates and complementary firewood) that visitors can reserve through the Wisconsin Union.

Pause at the tip of the point for a panoramic view of Lake Mendota, Madison's largest lake, then follow the path as it makes (nearly) a 180-degree turn and continues down the opposite side of the point. Around the 1-mile mark, retrace your route as you walk through the Narrows, passing a fire circle and an old-fashioned pump that offers drinking water. At 1.1 miles, leave some of the crowds behind and veer right to follow the trail that hugs the lakeshore. You'll pass a small sandy beach and public restrooms. The rest of the route will be noticeably quieter except for the sound of waves. For about a quarter mile, the trail crosses between the lake and a small marsh. Look for migrating birds here in the spring and fall.

Just before the trail heads into the woods at 1.5 miles, you'll see a large brick building beside a secluded beach. The Picnic Point Beach House, as it's known, is a humble storage building today, but in 1968, it was built to provide changing facilities and restrooms for swimmers. It never opened, however, because severe algae blooms at that time soon discouraged any would-be swimmers.

The next section of this route is my favorite: For 1.5 miles, the trail travels along and above the lake through a peaceful maple and oak forest. When the wind is right, the only sounds you hear are crashing waves and rustling leaves. At the 1.8-mile mark, there's an easy-to-miss detour to the tip of Frautschi

A stroll to Picnic Point is a classic fall hike and local favorite.

Point, a small overlook with pine and spruce woodlands and archaeological sites. Follow the path back to the main trail from here and turn right to continue. After passing a couple of scenic overlooks, at the 2.4-mile mark, you'll reach this route's turnaround point at Raymer's Cove. At the edge of the parking lot, steps lead down to the cove itself.

From the Raymer's Cove parking lot, retrace your path to the Big Oak Trail junction at the 2.8-mile mark. Turn right (south) onto Big Oak Trail, then stay straight at the next intersection. Depending on the season, the Big Oak Trail can become quite overgrown, but after about a quarter mile of dense canopy, a prairie comes into view. The trail emerges from the woods at the edge of Eagle Heights Community Gardens and to the east, Biocore Prairie. The latter is a long-term research and restoration project run by Biocore students and staff from the university.

After exiting the woods, turn left (east) and follow the mowed trail along the prairie's northern edge. At 3.2 miles, veer right (south) at the fork, then keep right again whenever another trail branches to the left. As the trail climbs alongside the prairie, be sure to turn around for a stunning view of Lake Mendota to the north. Turn left (east) at 3.4 miles and head back toward the woods, where a gravel service road turns right.

For the final quarter mile of the hike, the trail passes through Bill's Woods, an ongoing woodland restoration where volunteers are replacing invasive plants with native species. The woods are also ideal owl habitat; I've heard both barred and great horned owls here at dusk. After the trail crosses a service road at 3.5 miles, you're nearly done. Keep heading south, and in a few hundred yards you'll be back at the Picnic Point entrance.

GO FARTHER

With more than 12 miles of hiking trails and three main trailheads, a hike at Lakeshore Nature Preserve can be (nearly) as long or as short as you'd like. If you feel like going the distance, try an out-and-back day hike that links the Howard Temin Path (Trail 1), a few Picnic Point trails, and Eagle Heights Woods (Trail 3).

3 Lakeshore Nature Preserve: Eagle Heights Woods

DISTANCE:	1.3 miles
ELEVATION GAIN:	140 feet
HIGH POINT:	990 feet
DIFFICULTY:	Easy to moderate
FITNESS:	Walkers, hikers
FAMILY FRIENDLY:	Yes; some steeper sections more suitable for older children
DOG FRIENDLY:	Leashed dogs only
AMENITIES:	Parking lot
CONTACT/MAP:	Lakeshore Nature Preserve (UW–Madison); map available online and on-site
GPS:	N 43°5'20.0" W 89°26'22.7"
BEFORE YOU GO:	There are no restroom facilities or drinking water near this hike, so be sure to plan ahead.

GETTING THERE

Public Transit: Madison Metro Route 80 has stops along Lake Mendota Drive near Eagle Heights Woods.

Driving: From University Avenue in Madison, turn north onto University Bay Drive. Drive for 0.9 mile, then turn left onto

Daisy fleabane grows along the lakeside trail from Raymer's Cove.

Lake Mendota Drive. Follow Lake Mendota Drive for 0.8 mile until you see the Raymer's Cove parking lot on your right.

There are few places in Madison where the landscape has remained unchanged by plow or bulldozer. Perched on a bluff above Lake Mendota, Eagle Heights Woods is one of those rare locations. At 28 acres, this small but mighty forest ecosystem is much like it was generations ago. Red and white oak dominate the forest here, growing alongside other hardwoods like hickories. In a clearing near the top of a bluff lie burial mounds—one circular and two linear—that were constructed by Indigenous people more than one thousand years ago. Far removed from the busier areas of the Lakeshore Nature Preserve but still near campus, Eagle Heights Woods is the place to come for quiet.

GET MOVING

Trails are short in Eagle Heights Woods, but you can link them together with a Raymer's Cove connector for a 1.3-mile hike. Begin at the Raymer's Cove parking lot. Take the stairs down to the sheltered beach on Lake Mendota. Cross the beach and follow the trail as it veers right and climbs steeply out of the cove. Then continue following the trail along the lakefront. At the first trail intersection, turn left (south) and head toward Lake Mendota Drive. Watch for cars and bike traffic as you cross the road, and find the trail as it enters the woods on the other side. Keep left here as two trails branch right, one after the other.

The trail climbs through oak woods alongside a ridge for nearly a half mile. Through the trees below on your left, you'll see Eagle Heights Apartments, a large university housing community. Continue straight at the 0.4-mile mark when a trail branches right. Not long after, you'll pass two connector trails on the left that lead to the Eagle Heights neighborhood. Keep straight here to stay on route.

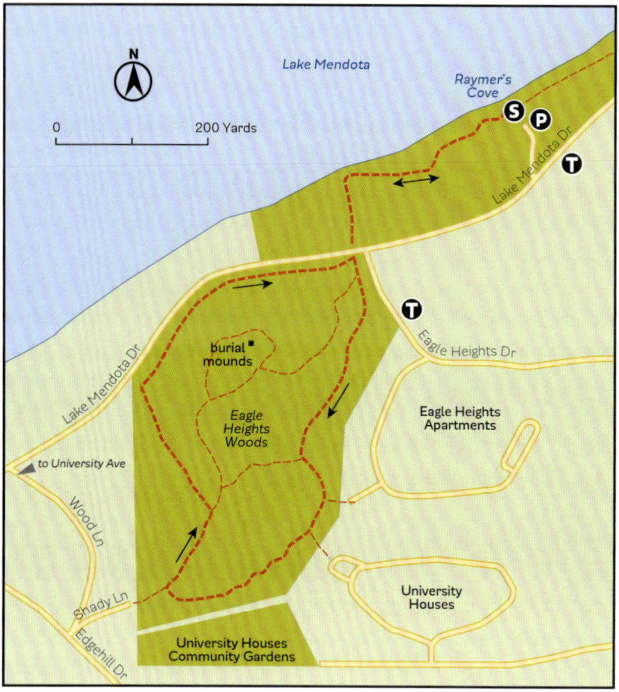

You'll reach the southern end of the main trail loop at 0.6 mile. At this point, another connector path heads left into the neighborhood, but to continue the hike, turn right (north). Look for woodland wildflowers as the trail continues a slow climb north. In spring, it's common to see trilliums and wild geraniums in bloom along these paths. If you want to take a detour to observe the burial mounds, your chance comes at the 0.7-mile mark, where a trail branches right and heads to the top of the bluff. It makes a small loop before returning to the connector trail. (There are also two other connector trails branching off the loop in other directions.) As you hike around the border of the mounds, be sure to stay on the trail. Depending on the season, the mounds can be difficult to see through all the understory plants.

Whether or not you take the bluff-top detour, continue north from the trail intersection at the 0.7-mile mark. The trail parallels Lake Mendota Drive to complete the main loop at 1.1 miles. From here, cross Lake Mendota Drive and retrace your route back to the Raymer's Cove parking lot.

GO FARTHER

After finishing the Eagle Heights Woods loop, you can easily hop on another trail at the Raymer's Cove parking lot. Follow the trail that leaves from the northwest corner of the lot for an additional out-and-back hike along the lakeshore (the distance is up to you) or continue all the way to Picnic Point by following the route described in Trail 2.

4 UW Arboretum: Grady Tract

DISTANCE: 3.7 miles
ELEVATION GAIN: 220 feet
HIGH POINT: 1010 feet
DIFFICULTY: Easy
FITNESS: Walkers, hikers, runners
FAMILY FRIENDLY: Yes
DOG FRIENDLY: Dogs not allowed
AMENITIES: None
CONTACT/MAP: University of Wisconsin–Madison Arboretum; map available online
GPS: N 43°2'3.0 W 89°26'36.2"
BEFORE YOU GO: Ecological restoration work is nearly always in progress at the Arboretum. Stay on the trails and heed any closures.

GETTING THERE

Public Transit: Madison Metro Route 18 stops near the intersection of Seminole Highway and Beltline Frontage Road.

Driving: From westbound Beltline Highway (Highway 12), take the Seminole Highway (exit 258A) and turn left (south). From eastbound Beltline Highway, take Todd Drive (exit 259), then turn right (west) on Beltline Frontage Road to reach the intersection with Seminole Highway in about a half mile. The trailhead parking lot is at the southeast corner of Seminole Highway and Beltline Frontage Road.

Don't be put off by the unassuming appearance of the tiny parking lot bordered by a chain-link fence. This is the trailhead for one of Madison's hidden gems: UW Arboretum's Grady Tract, 200 acres of woods, oak savanna, and prairie. The Arboretum is a favorite destination for hikers, runners, cyclists, and photographers, but most visitors to this botanical refuge never stray south of the Beltline. That's possibly because Madison's busiest roadway cuts off the Grady Tract from the main Arboretum. But if you know where to look, there's a pedestrian tunnel that links the two parcels—in addition to the easy-to-miss trailhead on Seminole Highway. As you step through the gate into the Grady Tract and leave the traffic behind, you may be surprised by how quickly the roar of the city gives way to a soothing forest sanctuary.

GET MOVING

There are many trails within the Grady Tract, but for a longer hike that takes you through the "secret" tunnel under the highway, follow this 3.7-mile route; it winds through the Grady Tract and then Noe Woods in the main Arboretum so you can experience the best of both worlds.

From the Grady Tract parking lot, head south into the Evjue Pines (a stand of stately white, red, and jack pines) and follow the trail that branches right. Like most trails here, it's a wide two-track. For nearly a mile, it parallels Seminole Highway, separated by dense trees the whole way. As you hike, continue heading straight (south) as three different trails branch to the left (east). At 0.6 mile, follow the trail as it makes an abrupt left turn and heads into the open. A chain-link fence marking the tract's southern boundary will be on the right.

At 0.8 mile, the trail takes another sharp turn to the left (north) as it traces the border between the forest and the sweeping Greene Prairie to the east. This 47-acre restored prairie was named for Henry Greene, the botanist who nearly single-handedly re-created it from depleted cornfields beginning in the 1940s. You'll have several more opportunities to view Greene's handiwork—and the more than two hundred native plant species that grow here—from other vantage points along the route. For the next half mile, the trail meanders through an in-progress restoration of oak savanna and prairie habitat. In early summer, look for the purple, spike-shaped clusters of wild lupine. (This native wildflower is the only host plant for the endangered Karner blue butterfly.) Along this section, keep right when a trail branches to the left, then turn right at the next T intersection. At 1.3 miles, continue straight at the four-way intersection, then continue straight again when another path veers left. For the next half mile or so, keep left when two more trails branch to the right. (The second will take you to one of the tract's southern trailheads in a residential neighborhood.)

At this point, the trail leaves the prairie behind and travels under the trees again. At 1.7 and 1.8 miles, continue straight (north) when you pass two connector trails on the left (west). The rumble of traffic will grow louder as you near the Beltline Highway, and soon you'll see the road itself in an opening in the trees ahead. As you step out of the woods, look for the entrance to the pedestrian tunnel under the highway. Follow the trail left and then make a quick right to reach it. The tunnel is tall enough that most people can walk through it without ducking, but watch your head anyway. Its concrete floor is often wet, so tread carefully.

When you exit the tunnel's north end, you'll navigate a narrow gate back onto Arboretum land. You're now in Noe Woods, a 40-acre oak forest with trees that are more than 150 years old. Head left at the fork and heed the poison ivy warning. For the next half mile, keep bearing left as the trail loops through the forest, passing under pines planted in honor of conservationist Aldo Leopold, the Arboretum's first

The Grady Tract is 200 acres of woods, oak savanna, and prairie.

research director. When the trail reaches a four-way intersection at 2.7 miles, continue straight. About 0.1 mile later, turn right (south) to follow the trail back into the woods, staying left at the next junction. After a quarter mile, you will reach another trail intersection. Turn right (south) and soon return to pass through the highway tunnel and head right. At 3.2 miles, turn left (south) into the woods and away from the highway. (For a shorter, more direct route back to the trailhead, continue hiking straight west instead.) When you reach a trail intersection at 3.4 miles, continue straight (west) for a few hundred feet until you see another trail branch off to the right (northwest). Follow this short connector trail back to the trailhead.

MAKE IT SHORTER

If you're short on time or have little ones in tow, try a simple out-and-back hike in the Grady Tract. Start at the Grady Tract trailhead and follow the trail to the right as it parallels Seminole Highway. Where the route turns left (east) at 0.6 mile, simply turn around and retrace your steps back to the trailhead. The total roundtrip distance will be around 1.3 miles.

5 UW Arboretum: Central Loop

DISTANCE: 2.4 miles
ELEVATION GAIN: 90 feet
HIGH POINT: 900 feet
DIFFICULTY: Easy
FITNESS: Walkers, hikers, trail runners
FAMILY FRIENDLY: Yes
DOG FRIENDLY: Dogs not allowed

AMENITIES: Visitor center, parking lot, restrooms, interpretative info, benches

CONTACT/MAP: University of Wisconsin–Madison Arboretum; map available online and on-site

GPS: N 43°2'26.2" W 89°25'50.8"

BEFORE YOU GO: The trails and parking lots at the UW Arboretum are free and open to the public. Grounds are open from 4:00 AM to 10:00 PM, and the Arboretum Visitor Center is open weekdays (9:30 to 4 PM) and weekends (12:30 to 4:00 PM).

GETTING THERE

Public Transit: The nearest Madison Metro bus stop is about a quarter mile from the Arboretum's west entrance. Take Madison Metro Route D2 to the intersection of Nakoma Road and Seminole Highway. Head south on Seminole Highway for 0.3 mile to the Arboretum's entrance, where it's another mile along a road to the visitor center.

Driving: The visitor center parking lot and main trailhead can be reached via two separate entrances. *From the west:* Take US Highway 12 west to Seminole Highway (exit 258A). Turn right (north) on Seminole Highway and continue for 0.3 mile to the entrance on your right. *From the east:* Take South Park Street to Haywood Avenue. Head west on Haywood for 0.2 mile until you reach the Arboretum's east entrance. Note: A gate at the visitor center prevents thru-traffic except for limited hours on Sundays.

Every spring, the grounds of the UW Arboretum turn into a fairytale garden of flowering trees: magnolia blooms the size of teacups, crab apple trees frosted with pink blossoms, and mazes of fragrant lilacs. You can't blame the camera-toting crowds who visit during this season; in April and May, the visitor parking lots are always full. But with its varied landscapes and abundant flora and fauna, the Arboretum is a beautiful place to visit any time of year—and these 1200 acres along Lake Wingra offer more than scenery. Since its

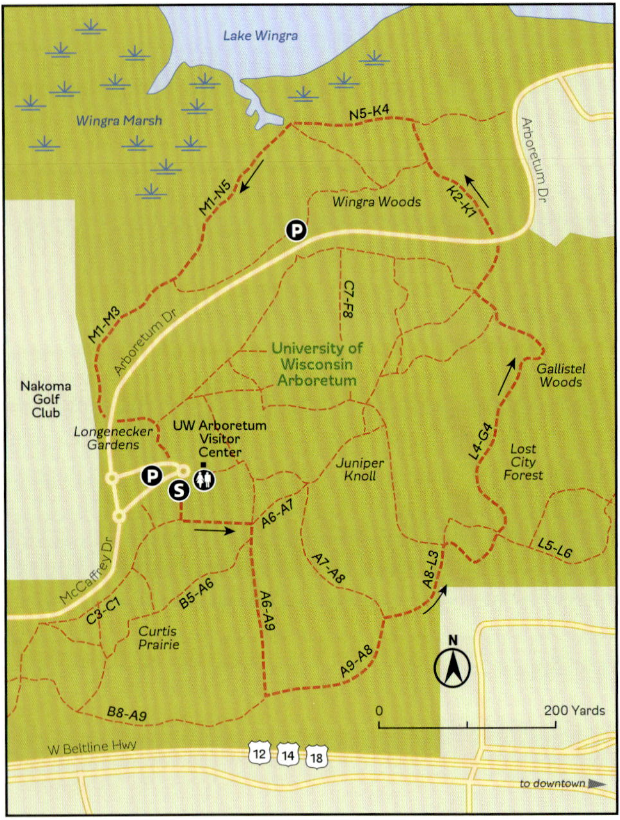

founding in 1934, the Arboretum has been a research center and leader in ecological restoration work. So, while it's a place that's well-known and well-loved for its gardens (i.e., the pretty flowering trees), the Arboretum's work extends beyond the furthest flowering tree and into the surrounding prairies, savannas, forests, wetlands, and lakeshore—and there are 17 miles of hiking trails to help you explore it. Stop at the Arboretum Visitor Center before or after a hike for information on their educational programs, volunteer opportunities, and guided walks. There's also an on-site nature-themed bookstore.

GET MOVING

For an overview of the Arboretum's landscapes, try this 2.4-mile loop that takes you through the world's oldest prairie restoration and some woodlands, with scenic stops at Lake Wingra's freshwater springs and Longenecker Horticultural Gardens. Head south from the visitor parking lot toward Curtis Prairie, where a mowed trail disappears into the grasses beside a metal sculpture by artist Glenn Wolf. This 70-acre tallgrass prairie restoration began more than eighty years ago. It's worth pausing to appreciate how the degraded soil of this former farm field was restored to a thriving grassland. A few dozen yards into the prairie, turn left (east) where the mowed trail intersects a gravel two-track trail. A few hundred yards beyond, turn right (south) onto another gravel two-track. You'll notice traffic noise from US Highway 12 (if you haven't already); it's just beyond the forest at the Arboretum's southern border. At 0.4 mile, turn left at the T intersection. The young maple and oak forest that grows along this trail section is beautiful in summer and fall—and provides welcome shade during warm-weather hikes.

When you reach a three-way trail intersection at 0.6 mile, turn right (east) and you'll soon cross a concrete spillway used for stormwater management. (Unless it has recently rained, the spillway should be dry.) At 0.8 mile, follow the narrow trail that branches off the main path to the right for a short jaunt through dense forest and understory. You'll emerge from these woods at a four-way intersection. Head straight (north) to continue into the Arboretum's Lost City Forest. An interpretative sign explains the story behind this cryptic name: Before the Arboretum acquired the land,

The UW Arboretum's magnolias, crab apples, and lilacs draw crowds every spring.

it was the proposed site of an elaborate 1920s subdivision. Only five homes were built before financial woes and construction issues ended the project.

Today, Lost City Forest is the site of ongoing ecological restoration as volunteers create a more open forest canopy. You may spot brush piles and felled trees during your hike. In autumn, this forest is alive with the constant rustling and chattering of squirrels and chipmunks. After a half-mile trek through Lost City Forest, you'll cross into Gallistel Woods, where more than one thousand maple, basswood, and beech seedlings were planted sixty years ago. In autumn, this forest glows bright with golden leaves above and below.

At 1.3 miles, turn right and you'll shortly reach the Arboretum's main road. It can be busy with cars, bikes, and pedestrians, so watch for traffic before crossing at the crosswalk. The trail then dives into Wingra Woods, a forest of oaks, hemlocks, and sugar maples. Stay straight when another trail enters from the left at 1.5 miles. As you draw nearer to Lake Wingra, listen for the otherworldly call of sandhill cranes.

At 1.6 miles, turn left at the T intersection. For the next quarter mile, this wooded trail parallels the marsh at Lake Wingra's western end, passing several freshwater springs. There were once nearly forty freshwater springs along Lake Wingra; sadly, all but fourteen have been destroyed by development. The ones that remain, while scenic, have been contaminated by chloride due to excessive road salt use. To protect what's left of these fragile springs, admire them from a distance. The largest of these, Big Spring, is at the 1.8-mile mark and is an oasis for wildlife throughout the year because its waters don't freeze.

At 2 miles, stay straight when a connector trail veers left into the prairie. Through the woods on the right, you'll glimpse Nakoma Golf Club. A few hundred yards later, exit the woods and cross the Arboretum's main road using the crosswalk. You'll now be in Longenecker Gardens (aka, the flowering trees section of the Arboretum). From here, there's no discernible trail, so it's a choose-your-own- adventure ramble back to your parking lot starting point. Simply head in a southeast direction through the crab apple and magnolia trees and keep an eye out for the visitor center—and the roving band of wild turkeys that makes their home here.

MAKE IT SHORTER

For an easy stroll, especially with young children, go for a walk through the Longenecker Horticultural Gardens. There aren't any trails, but there are several benches and it's easy to pick your own route through the grassy open areas and under the trees.

6 Turville Point Conservation Park

DISTANCE:	1.8 miles
ELEVATION GAIN:	130 feet
HIGH POINT:	900 feet
DIFFICULTY:	Easy
FITNESS:	Walkers, hikers, runners
FAMILY FRIENDLY:	Yes
DOG FRIENDLY:	Dogs are not allowed at Turville Point Conservation Park or near the beach or playground at Olin Park.
AMENITIES:	Restrooms, parking lot, drinking water, boat launch, picnic tables, swimming beach, playground, event pavilion (all at Olin Park)
CONTACT/MAP:	City of Madison Parks Division; map available online
GPS:	N 43°3'7.4" W 89°22'34.9"

GETTING THERE

Public Transit: Madison Metro Route O stops near Rimrock Road and John Nolen Drive, where it's a half mile to the

Turville Bay trailhead. From Rimrock Road, cross John Nolen Drive at the signal, then follow the paved bike path left (north) to the trailhead parking lot.

Driving: From US Highway 12 in Madison (from either direction), take the exit for John Nolen Drive (exit 263). Head north for 0.8 mile and then turn right on Olin-Turville Court. The Turville Bay trailhead is at the first parking lot on your right (which is also a trailhead for the Capital City Trail, a popular biking route.)

Turville Point Conservation Park and adjacent Olin Park cover more than 100 acres along Lake Monona, providing postcard-perfect views of Madison's downtown. Olin Park—with its public boat launch, picnic areas, and historical pavilion—is a popular event venue year-round that's especially busy

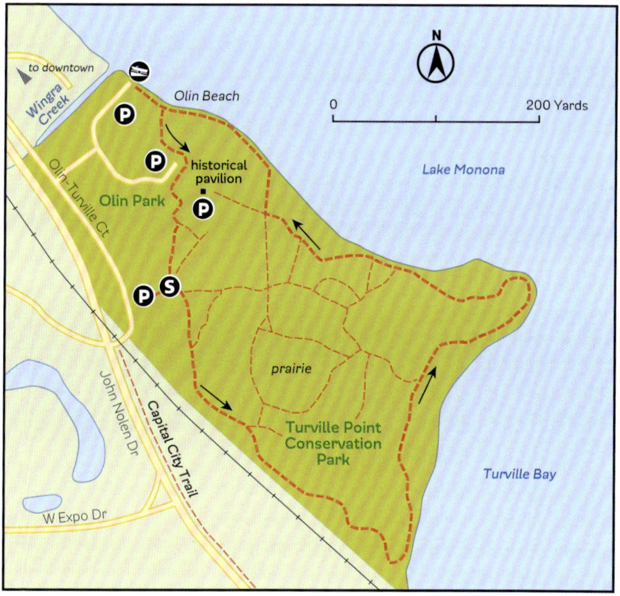

The outer loop at Turville Point Conservation Park

during the summer months (though many locals know the park for its annual holiday lights display in December). Turville Point is Olin's quieter neighbor. A former farm that once belonged to the Turville family, the park's 60-some acres of woods, shoreline, and prairie is an ecological restoration project that's crisscrossed with hiking trails. You may even witness one of the park's more unique ecological projects during your hike: grazing goats. Since 2020, Madison's parks division has hired goats from a local farmer to control invasive species like buckthorn and honeysuckle—a better (and more endearing) alternative to herbicide.

GET MOVING

Turville Point Conservation Park has one main trail that circles the point, with several connector trails and smaller loops within it. For a 1.8-mile hike that includes the outer trail and a foray to the adjacent Olin Park lakefront, start at the Turville Point trailhead. Take the trail right (south) in a counterclockwise direction through the woods, staying right at the first junction. The noisiest part of the hike will be on the west side of the point, due to traffic and, at times, outdoor events at the nearby Alliant Energy Center. At 0.2 mile, a connector trail veers left, then takes a sharp left to reach the Prairie Loop trail. Take this path if you want to see the small prairie in the center of Turville Point. (This path also serves as a shortcut to the lake side of the point.)

To stay on the recommended route, continue hiking the main trail; after another half mile, you'll glimpse Lake Monona glinting through the trees. Keep following the trail as it turns left, and at 0.8 mile, you'll have your first opportunity to walk to the water's edge along Turville Bay. From here to Olin Park, you'll stay right at all junctions. In summer, the bay can be full of white water lilies, a native aquatic plant. It's also a popular fishing spot for people and wildlife alike—watch for great blue herons fishing in the shallows.

The trail briefly heads away from the shoreline into the trees before returning to the lake at the 1-mile mark. Here on the lake side of the point, you'll have several chances to see

Madison's picturesque skyline across the water, but depending on the season and water quality, you may not always want to linger. Unfortunately, Madison's lakes are plagued with ongoing water-quality issues, including toxic blue-green algae. As a result, this section of the trail can sometimes have a very unpleasant smell. After following the lakeshore for about a quarter mile, the trail heads back into the woods. With a canopy of mature oaks all around, there's an active population of gray squirrels and chipmunks stirring up the leaves below and announcing your presence with warning calls.

At the intersection at 1.2 miles, continue straight (northwest). Just beyond this point is where you'll leave Turville Point Conservation Park and circle through Olin Park. (You can also turn left at this intersection to head directly back to the Turville Point trailhead.) While Olin Park doesn't have any hiking trails, it's worth taking a short walk through it for more lake views. At the next intersection, turn right toward the lake. At 1.3 miles, the trail ends at a mowed lawn. From this point, continue hiking northwest across the lawn along the lake to Olin Beach. The beach is small and there's no lifeguard on duty, but it offers another opportunity to get near the lake and snag some photos of the scenery. After reaching the boat launch at 1.5 miles, turn around and follow the paved bike path south toward the historical pavilion. At the parking lot in front of the pavilion, follow the path that goes past the playground to the mowed walking trail beyond, which will return you to the parking lot for Turville Point and the Capital City Trail.

GO FARTHER

Return to Turville Point in winter—and bring your skis. When there's enough snow, the park offers more than two miles of hiking trails groomed for (classic) cross-country skiing—no ski pass required.

7 Owen Conservation Park

DISTANCE:	1.4 miles
ELEVATION GAIN:	150 feet
HIGH POINT:	1080 feet
DIFFICULTY:	Easy
FITNESS:	Walkers, hikers
FAMILY FRIENDLY:	Yes
DOG FRIENDLY:	Dogs not allowed
AMENITIES:	Restrooms, parking lot, picnic tables, interpretative info
CONTACT/MAP:	City of Madison Parks Division; map available online and on-site
GPS:	N 43°4'22.7" W 89°29'14.4"
BEFORE YOU GO:	Plant and animal habitat take priority at this conservation park; rules differ from other city parks (for instance, no dogs allowed).

GETTING THERE

Public Transit: Madison Metro Route 8 and Route 15 from downtown stop at Old Middleton Road and North Rosa Road. From there, walk west on Old Sauk Road for about a half mile to the park entrance (6021 Old Sauk Road).

Driving: From downtown Madison, head west on University Avenue to Whitney Way. Turn left (south) on South Whitney Way, then take your first right on Old Middleton Road. After about half a mile, take a slight left onto Old Sauk Road. After another half mile, turn left into the park and drive another half mile to reach the parking lot and trailhead. Note: The park isn't often busy, but there can be traffic during drop-off and pick-up at the elementary school across the road.

From the Beltline (US Highway 12) heading west, take the exit for Old Sauk Road. Turn right (east) onto Old Sauk Road. After 1.8 miles, the park entrance will be on your

The prairie at Owen Park attracts pollinators like the eastern tiger swallowtail.

right. Turn right into the park and drive another half mile to reach the parking lot and trailhead.

In this quiet westside neighborhood, a narrow driveway disappears into a tunnel of trees. Follow it, and the woods soon open into sunny prairie as you pass an old white farmhouse. Owen Conservation Park was once the summertime retreat and farm of UW professor Edward T. Owen, but today this nearly 100-acre greenspace is a public park managed by the City of Madison. More than 3 miles of hiking trails wind through these peaceful 40 acres of deciduous forest and more than 50 acres of prairie. Most of the trails are easy, especially the wide, mowed trails in the park's prairie. Wildflowers fill the meadows and woods during summer, as do migrating songbirds. No matter the season, you'll likely spot the local flock of wild turkeys. And if you linger here

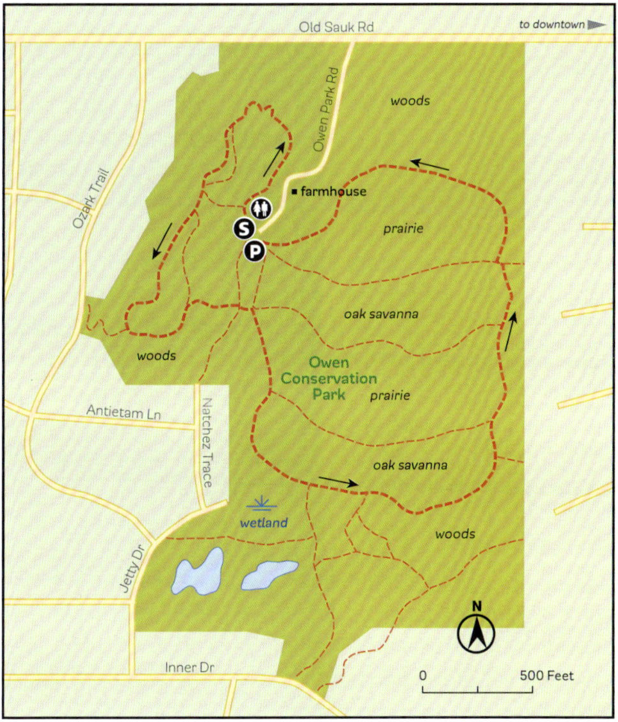

until just before dusk (when the park closes), you may hear a barred owl or two.

GET MOVING

For a 1.4-mile hike that takes you through the park's woods and prairie, start at the trailhead to the left of the public restrooms. A few steps in, take a right at the T intersection and follow the trail up into the woods. The trail makes a quarter-mile loop around a small hill, staying in the woods the whole way. In spring and summer, look for woodland wildflowers like large-flowered trillium, a white three-petaled flower, growing on the forest floor.

Before the trail loops back to the T intersection at the beginning, you'll reach another intersection at 0.2 mile. Stay straight to continue the hike, or turn left to return to the trailhead. Stay straight when another trail branches left. For another quarter mile, the trail loops through the woods. At 0.4 mile, stay left when a spur trail branches to the right leading into the neighborhood. Several paces later, keep right when another trail branches left. At 0.5 mile, you'll reach two consecutive trail intersections. Stay straight at the first, and turn right (south) at the second. To the east, the land slopes away into sunny prairie and oak savanna. They're not always visible at the height of summer, but the grasses and wildflowers hide several mowed hiking trails. Follow the outer 0.9-mile loop to circle the perimeter of the prairie and return to the trailhead. Three parallel trails (about 0.2 mile each) cut through the center of the prairie if you need a shortcut.

GO FARTHER

If you want to hike all 3 miles of the park's trails (and then some), there are a few short, interconnected trails at the southern end of the park. Four of these trails will eventually lead you out of the park and into the neighborhood, but it's easy enough to turn around and find your way back.

8 Monona Lake Loop: Olin Park

DISTANCE:	4.2 miles
ELEVATION GAIN:	60 feet
HIGH POINT:	870 feet
DIFFICULTY:	Easy
FITNESS:	Walkers, runners
FAMILY FRIENDLY:	Yes
DOG FRIENDLY:	Leashed dogs only
AMENITIES:	Parking lot, restrooms, drinking water, beach, playground, benches, boat launch
CONTACT/MAP:	Monona East Side Business Alliance; map available online
GPS:	N 43°3'17.8" W 89°22'42.0"

GETTING THERE

Public Transit: The easiest way to access this route by public transit is to hike the route in reverse and begin at B.B. Clarke Beach rather than Olin Park. Madison Metro Route 38 has stops along Jenifer Street at the southwest end of B.B. Clarke Beach.

Driving: From US Highway 12 in Madison (either direction), take the exit for John Nolen Drive (exit 263). Head north for 0.8 mile and then turn right on Olin-Turville Court. The boat launch parking lot (this route's starting point) will be the second parking lot on the right. Note: Given its proximity to downtown and the Alliant Energy Center, there can be traffic en route to Olin Park, particularly during rush hour or special events.

The Monona Lake Loop is a 13-mile bike route that circles Lake Monona. Although popular among cyclists and runners, many miles are also ideal for hikers, walkers, wheelchair users, and anyone pushing a stroller with little ones

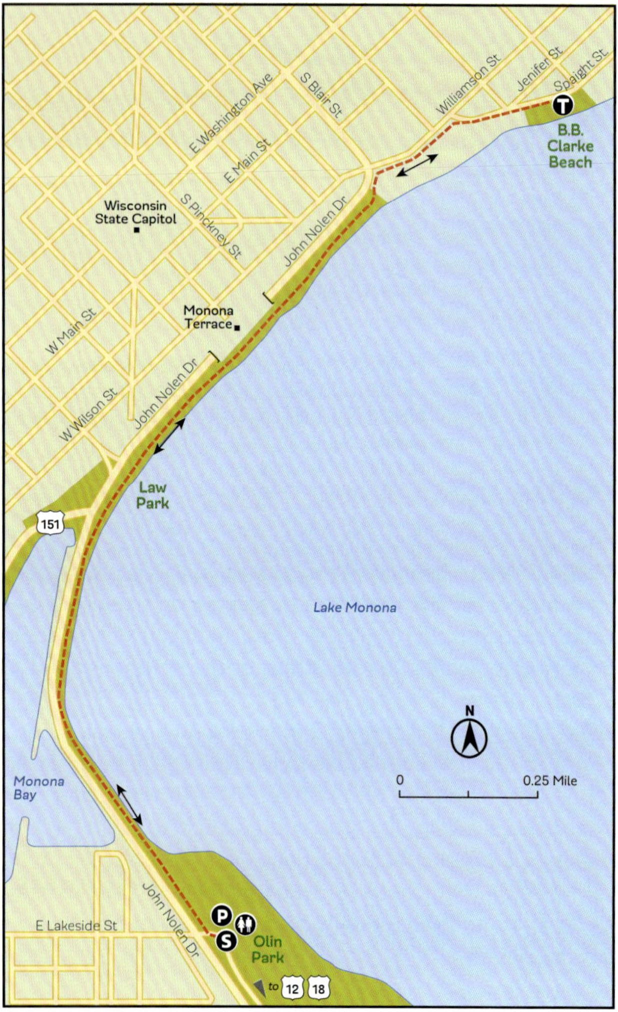

in tow. The route is a mix of paved bike paths and city streets that often lack a shoulder, so not all sections are pedestrian friendly or easy to navigate. But if you're looking for a truly

Downtown Madison's skyline is a highlight of the Monona Lake Loop.

urban hike with lake views and interesting stops, this is it. Unless you're in the mood for a half marathon, choose a short segment to hike. One of the route's most pedestrian-friendly sections begins at Olin Park and offers an incredible view of downtown Madison across the lake. Walk this stretch as an out-and-back for a roundtrip of 4.2 miles. (Or turn around sooner for a shorter hike.) Many cyclists use this path, so watch for other trail users and keep to one side.

GET MOVING

Begin at Olin Park and follow the paved Capital City Trail as it departs from the park's northwest end and parallels John Nolen Drive. This is one of the busiest thoroughfares

WINTER HIKING

Nature doesn't close when the leaves and temperatures drop. While many people prefer to hike in spring, summer, or fall in Wisconsin, there are reasons to keep hiking all year long. Winter can be an especially peaceful time on the trails, giving you the opportunity to see a familiar landscape in a new way. Nearly all local hiking trails are open in winter, but some are groomed for cross-country skiing or are open to snowshoeing. Research your destination ahead of time and heed any closures you see at the trailhead; some ski and snowshoe trails are closed to hikers. If they're open to hikers, be sure to walk along the edge of the trail and not on the groomed section, and yield to other trail users. Here are more winter hiking tips:

- **Layer up.** Wear a base layer (top and bottom) made from a synthetic fabric. Then add additional layers of clothing based on the temperature and weather forecast.
- **Wear waterproof boots or shoes.** Even when there isn't snow, trails can be muddy, and nothing ruins a hike (at least for me) like wet, cold feet.
- **Bring a hat, gloves, and extra socks.** If you don't wear a hat and gloves, at least bring them along in your pockets or pack. And if your socks get wet, you'll appreciate an extra pair.
- **Try trekking poles.** Some hikers prefer to use trekking poles year-round, but they can be especially helpful on icy or muddy winter terrain.
- **Check the forecast.** Know the temperature, windchill, and precipitation chances before you go, but always bring more clothing than you think you'll need.
- **Pack water, snacks, and a hot drink.** The water and snacks will keep you hydrated and fueled, and the hot drink will warm you up—it's also a great reward at the end of a cold hike.

in Madison, so the traffic is loud along this stretch—but on the upside, it offers clear views of Lake Monona and downtown. Around the 1-mile mark, the path enters Law Park, a narrow greenspace along the lakefront where you can watch the local water-ski team's free shows on summer Sundays. With cars zooming past and downtown buildings ahead, you may be surprised to learn that this spot is known for one of the city's most intriguing wildlife sightings. Snowy owls, flying in from the Arctic, sometimes make an appearance here in winter when the frozen lake resembles the tundra. They've even been photographed perching placidly on the tops of streetlights above John Nolen Drive.

Next the route passes between the lake and Monona Terrace, a convention center first designed by Frank Lloyd Wright in the 1930s but not built until 1997. Take a detour (via the stairs) to the Terrace's rooftop gardens for an even better view of the lake, or stop at the outdoor Lake Vista Café. Back down below, the paved path continues alongside John Nolen Drive before it intersects Williamson Street at the 1.7-mile mark. Follow the path as it turns right at Williamson, also known as Willy Street. After a couple hundred yards, follow the sidewalk to turn right onto Jenifer Street. Next, veer right onto Spaight Street and follow the path into B.B. Clarke Beach, a small park with a sand swimming beach and playground. After you've had a chance to cool off or watch the waves, follow the route in reverse to return to Olin Park.

GO FARTHER

A hike on the Monona Lake Loop can be as long or as short as you'd like. Look at a map to find a section that interests you, and do another out-and-back hike.

Next page: The Yahara River near Westport before it flows into Lake Mendota (Trail 9)

NORTHEAST

Northeast Madison is where you'll find the city's largest public park and the county's largest wetland. The latter, the vast Cherokee Marsh, is the lifeblood of the region's lakes, as it filters fresh water into the north end of Lake Mendota. Spread over 2,000 acres and several tracts of public land, Cherokee Marsh is critical wildlife habitat, especially for resident and migratory birds. Hiking trails along the shoreline offer views of the marsh and abundant bird-watching opportunities. Continuing south along Lake Mendota, Governor's Island and Warner Park are both beautiful places to watch a sunset over the lake and explore a wooded path or two. Although residents may know Warner Park as home of the city's minor league baseball team, the Madison Mallards, it's also a haven for urban wildlife. In recent years, park visitors have even seen a family of beavers in the vicinity, a keystone species that's becoming increasingly important in climate change mitigation efforts. Five miles northwest of Warner Park, as the crane flies, is Token Creek County Park. This huge park has a creekside hiking trail, along with a campground, dog park, and disc golf course.

9 Cherokee Marsh Natural Resource Area

DISTANCE:	3.8 miles
ELEVATION GAIN:	130 feet
HIGH POINT:	900 feet
DIFFICULTY:	Easy to moderate
FITNESS:	Walkers, hikers
FAMILY FRIENDLY:	Yes. Depending on the season and trail conditions, one wooded section can be especially narrow and overgrown.
DOG FRIENDLY:	Leashed dogs only; Dane County Parks dog permit required.
AMENITIES:	None
CONTACT/MAP:	Dane County Parks; map available online
GPS:	N 43°10'7.9" W 89°23'1.9"
BEFORE YOU GO:	Trails are open to both hiking and snowshoeing in winter; no permit is required for either activity.

GETTING THERE

Driving: From downtown Madison, head north on East Johnson Street to County Highway 113 North. Veer left (north) onto County Highway 113 North and continue for 5.8 miles. Turn right (east) onto West River Road. After 1.5 miles, the trailhead parking lot will be on your right.

Madison is known for its lakes, but its well-loved freshwater chain owes its continued existence to another, less-lauded habitat: Cherokee Marsh. At more than 2,000 acres, Cherokee Marsh is the largest wetland in Dane County, fed by the Yahara River and several smaller streams. Like most watery places, it's best explored by kayak, but there are also many miles of hiking trails along its shores.

The marsh is divided into several large tracts of public land, and their similar names can make it difficult to distinguish one area from another. Look at a map and you'll

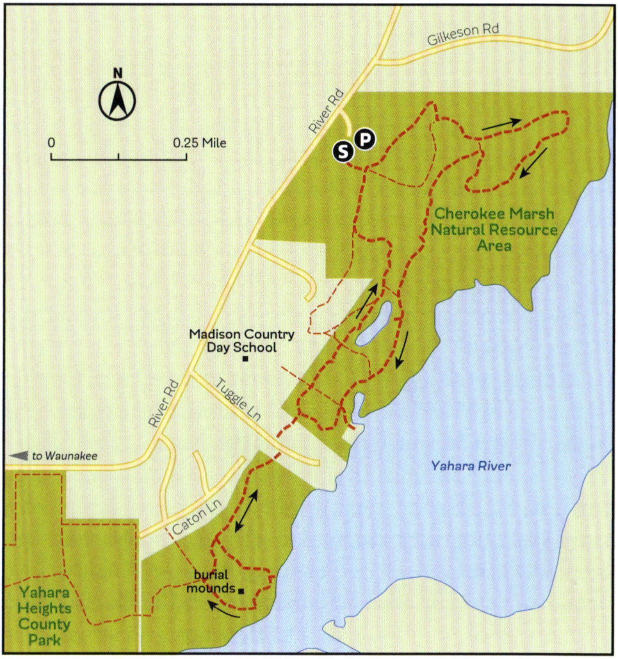

see Cherokee Marsh Natural Resource Area, Cherokee Marsh State Fishery Area, Cherokee Marsh State Natural Area, Cherokee Marsh Conservation Park (Mendota Unit), Cherokee Marsh Conservation Park (North Unit), Cherokee Marsh Conservation Park (South Unit), and lastly, Cherokee Marsh Wildlife Area. To complicate matters, not all tracts are linked by land, so determining the correct trailhead for your chosen hike is crucial. (That's where GPS coordinates and street addresses come in handy.) This hike begins and ends at Cherokee Marsh Natural Resource Area on the northwest side of the marsh, in Waunakee. It's a nearly 4-mile loop through woodlands and grassland habitat, with stops at a spring-fed pond and a couple of scenic overlooks.

GET MOVING

Follow the trail from the trailhead parking lot. Turn left at the first fork, hiking the boundary of the meadow and woods. At 0.3 mile, keep right when a connector trail veers left to a residential neighborhood. After a short march through the woods, the trail loops around a small field. At the 1-mile mark, turn left where a narrow trail enters the woods. You'll soon pass a wooden sign for "Domino's Trail." For nearly a half mile, the trail weaves through dense hickory and oak woods—you may have to navigate around a fallen tree or two. Around 1.4 miles, this narrow footpath links up to a wide, mowed trail. Turn left on the mowed trail, and just beyond the intersection, you'll glimpse a large pond to your right. A spur trail leads to a bench along the shore of this remarkably clear, spring-fed pond.

When you reach a trail intersection at 1.6 miles, stay straight. You'll soon pass through an open space that looks like an outdoor classroom with several benches. This area and others like it are used by Madison Country Day School, which is up the hill to the right. At 1.7 miles, turn left to take a short dead-end trail to the shore, where you can get a view of the Yahara River and surrounding marsh. Then return to the previous intersection and turn left (west) to continue the hike.

Turn left at 1.9 miles. This next section of the hike passes through private property, so stay on the trail and look for trail signage after you cross the road. As the trail parallels the Yahara River, you'll get longer views across the water, with more scenic overlooks at the end of the final loop. At 2.2 miles, turn left and head toward the water. At the next trail intersection, go left, then at the next, go right. About a quarter mile after the turn, follow a short trail to the water's edge, if you'd like; otherwise, continue on the route. At 2.5 miles, you'll pass the site of several Native American burial mounds noted by a sign. Burial mounds like these are protected by Wisconsin state law; stay on the designated trail

This crystal-clear pond is a popular local fishing spot.

to avoid damaging them. Beyond this area is a beautiful, shaded overlook of the Yahara River.

At 2.6 miles, turn right at the four-way trail intersection. Then continue straight at the next three-way intersection, and for the next 0.3 mile, retrace your route until you reach the prairie behind Madison Country Day School. Turn left when you reach the trail intersection at the 3-mile mark, and continue straight at the next intersection. This path will take you along the northwest side of the pond you passed earlier in the hike. At 3.3 miles, a small spur trail ends at the shore, where you'll see that local students have named it "Splendor & Glee Pond." From the pond, follow the trail north as it becomes a wide dirt path through the woods. At 3.6 miles, turn right; then turn left at the next intersection to return to your starting point.

GO FARTHER

Cherokee Marsh Natural Resource Area is adjacent to the 141-acre Yahara Heights County Park. To extend this hike by another 1.7 miles, follow the connector trail at the southern end of this route (at the 2.6-mile mark) and hike an out-and-back path through Yahara Heights County Park, returning to the original route where you left it.

10 Cherokee Marsh Conservation Park: North

DISTANCE: 3 miles
ELEVATION GAIN: 120 feet
HIGH POINT: 930 feet
DIFFICULTY: Easy to moderate
FITNESS: Hikers
FAMILY FRIENDLY: Yes
DOG FRIENDLY: Dogs not allowed
AMENITIES: Parking lot, restrooms, drinking water
CONTACT/MAP: City of Madison Parks Division; map available online and on-site
GPS: N 43°10'1.9" W 89°21'52.5"

GETTING THERE

Driving: From north Madison, take State Highway 113/Northport Drive to North Sherman Avenue and go north until it ends in the trailhead parking lot.

WILDLIFE

No matter which trail you choose in Madison, you'll hike through wildlife habitat—even in the heart of the city. Many animal species have adapted to living near people and can be seen in rural and urban areas alike.

Below I've listed wildlife you may encounter while hiking in the greater Madison area—I've seen or heard most of them myself. These lists don't include every animal species that live here, because there are simply too many. (In Dane County, there are more than one hundred species of butterflies!) Animals with an asterisk* are rare or rarely seen. For instance, there aren't many black bears in our area, but they are spotted from time to time. And coyotes, while quite common, prefer to avoid humans.

No matter which animals you encounter in your outdoor adventures, keep a respectful distance. Never feed wildlife or remove animals from their natural habitat. If you come across an injured or sick animal, contact the Dane County Humane Society's Wildlife Rehabilitation Center. Their staff can assess the situation and let you know what to do.

- **Birds:** American robins, northern cardinals, blue jays, red-winged blackbirds, sparrows (several species), woodpeckers (downy, red-bellied, red-headed, pileated), house finches, goldfinches, eastern bluebirds, sandhill cranes, Canada geese, wild turkeys, great blue herons, green herons, mallards, American crows, great horned owls, barred owls, European starlings, barn swallows, dark-eyed juncos, black-capped chickadees, white-breasted nuthatches, house wrens, mourning doves, Baltimore orioles, ruby-throated hummingbirds
- **Mammals:** squirrels (gray, red, and fox), chipmunks, beavers*, muskrats, ground squirrels and gophers, voles, mice, moles*, bats* (little brown, big brown), woodchucks, skunks*, opossums*, raccoons, badgers*, white-tailed deer, coyotes*, red foxes*, bobcats*, black bears*
- **Amphibians, Reptiles, and Lizards:** spring peepers, American toads, boreal chorus frogs, American bullfrogs, tree frogs (gray and Cope's gray), painted turtles, snapping turtles*, common garter snakes, red-bellied snakes, smooth green snakes
- **Insects:** butterflies (monarch, eastern tiger swallowtail, black swallowtail, cabbage white, spring azure); moths (Isabella tiger moth, white sphinx moth); spiders (garden, grass, orb weaver); bumblebees and bees (several species); fireflies

Cherokee Marsh Conservation Park includes the public lands along the southeast side of the Yahara River as it flows into Lake Mendota. The park is opposite Cherokee Marsh Natural Resource Area in Waunakee and is divided into three distinct "units" that are separated by residential neighborhoods and roads. The North Unit is the largest at nearly 1,000 acres of oak savanna, woodlands, and marsh, with more than four miles of winding trails. With such diverse habitat, the park offers year-round wildlife and bird-watching opportunities, and also hosts a free monthly Bird & Nature Adventures guided walk. (No registration is required; details are available on the park website.) Since several trails leave from the main trailhead, a hike here can be short or more meandering.

GET MOVING

For a 3-mile loop through woods, marsh, and prairie, follow the gravel service road that leaves from the northwest end of the parking lot. Turn right (north) when the road intersects the River Trail. At the next trail intersection at 0.1 mile, turn left (west). The wide, flat trail parallels the river for a bit, but it's difficult to see it through the trees. You'll soon get your chance at 0.2 mile, when a dead-end trail leads to an elevated platform. Climb a few steps to get a high view of the surrounding marsh and the Yahara River beyond. In December, you might even see snow-white tundra swans gathered here during their annual migration.

Continue hiking north, then turn right (east) at 0.3 mile onto the Overlook Trail. The trail narrows here and begins a steep climb through the forest for about a quarter mile before leveling out again. Reach a sunny scenic overlook at 0.5 mile where you can see prairie and wetlands to the north. Follow the route north—now a wide, mowed trail—as it descends from the overlook into the wetlands. Stay right at 0.7 mile when a trail veers left. Shortly afterward, another dead-end path will take you to a small pier overlooking a seasonal pond.

Keep left as the trail turns gradually to the south and passes two trails branching to the right. At 0.9 mile the trail passes fenced-off rock outcroppings that look like an old quarry. From here, the hike winds through marshland for a half mile or so, sometimes on a packed dirt trail, sometimes on aluminum boardwalk. Depending on the season, look and listen for sandhill cranes. At 1.2 miles, turn left onto a long stretch of boardwalk. In late summer, the grasses and sedges grow tall along it and echo with a constant chorus of insects. Veer right (south) at the next two trail forks. At the 1.6-mile mark, turn left at the T intersection, following signs for the Woodpecker Trail.

A boardwalk travels through marsh habitat.

Cross North Sherman Avenue, watching for traffic, and pick up the trail on the opposite side. Leaving the marsh behind, the gravel trail crosses through oak savanna. At 1.8 miles, turn right (west) at the trail intersection and head into the prairie. This stretch is full of wildflowers in the warmer months and is ideal habitat for eastern bluebirds, swallows, and song sparrows. Continue straight when a connector trail leaves the main trail on the left. Turn left when the Woodpecker Trail intersects with the Aspen Trail; then turn left again onto the River Trail. (A right on the Aspen Trail will take you directly back to the trailhead.)

At 2.5 miles, turn right (northwest) toward the river. This short out-and-back section of the hike is the best opportunity to get an up-close look at Cherokee Marsh. After passing a grove of trees, look for the boardwalk into the marsh. The boardwalk dead-ends at a bench that's surrounded by marsh grasses. It's a quiet spot for bird-watching or relaxing at the (almost) end of a hike. From the bench, retrace your route back to the last trail intersection and turn left. Around the 3-mile mark, you'll reach the gravel service road that leads back to the parking lot.

MAKE IT SHORTER

For a 1.2-mile hike that includes two scenic overlooks, follow the route instructions above until the trail junction at the 1-mile mark. Turn right (west) at this intersection to walk along the north edge of a prairie. At the next four-way trail intersection, turn left to follow the Bluebird Trail back to the gravel service road where you started.

11 Cherokee Marsh Conservation Park: South

DISTANCE: 1.2 miles
ELEVATION GAIN: 60 feet
HIGH POINT: 880 feet
DIFFICULTY: Easy
FITNESS: Walkers, hikers, runners
FAMILY FRIENDLY: Yes
DOG FRIENDLY: Dogs not allowed
AMENITIES: Parking lot, interpretative info, boat launch
CONTACT/MAP: City of Madison Parks Division; map available online
GPS: N 43°8'54.7" W 89°22'58.4"

GETTING THERE

Public Transit: Madison Metro Route L has stops along Wheeler Road. From the intersection of Wheeler Road and Delaware Boulevard, head west on Wheeler for 0.3 mile until you reach the park entrance; it will be on the north side of the road. You can access trails here or walk 0.4 mile down the park road to the boat launch parking lot and main trailhead.

The trail leads to a wide view of Cherokee Marsh.

Driving: From State Highway 113/Northport Drive in north Madison, turn north onto School Road. After 0.7 mile, just after School Road becomes Wheeler Road, turn left. Then take an immediate right into the parking lot.

Tucked between Cherokee Marsh and several neighborhoods, the south unit of Cherokee Marsh Conservation Park is not only critical habitat for native flora and fauna, it's a welcome nature retreat for city residents amid Madison's busy north side. Nearly 4 miles of easy trails wind through restored prairies, savannas, and woods. Unlike the park's other units, the south one offers access to the marsh itself, with a public boat launch and pier that are open to boaters and paddlers alike. In the colder months when there's enough snow, nearly all the park's trails are groomed for classic cross-country skiing—so exchange your hiking boots for a pair of skis if you plan to explore the trails in winter.

GET MOVING

Take in two of the park's eight named trails and enjoy the marsh views on a 1.2-mile stroll through woodland and prairie. Begin on the west side of the boat launch parking lot and follow the Sunset Trail into the woods. It briefly heads north up a hill before making a sharp turn to the south through the forest. When the trees are bare, as in early spring, this first quarter mile of the trail offers the best marsh views on the route; an overlook with a bench at 0.1 mile is a nice place to pause.

At 0.2 mile, keep right and follow the trail as it parallels the park's road. (The trail branching to the left circles back to the parking lot; you'll return on it later.) Follow the path to the right of a park maintenance building, then keep right to hike the Bluebird Hill Trail in a counterclockwise direction. Here the trail makes a loop around a little prairie before

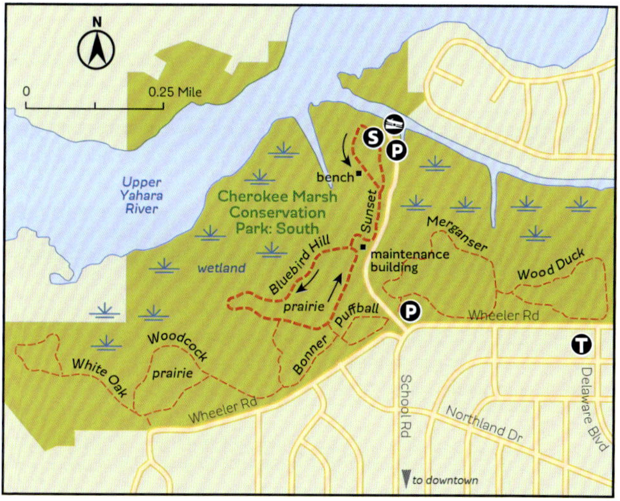

turning north and passing under trees. At the 0.7-mile mark, stay straight when the Bonner Trail turns right and then again when another trail branches right. Complete the Bluebird Hill Trail loop at 0.9 mile, and then retrace your route past the park maintenance building to the Sunset Trail loop. When you reach the trail fork at 1.1 miles, veer right through the woods to return to the trailhead.

GO FARTHER

For a hike that's twice as long, add the Bonner, Woodcock, and White Oak Trails to this route. At the 0.7-mile mark, instead of continuing on the Bluebird Hill Trail, turn right (south) onto the Bonner Trail. This will link you to the Woodcock and White Oak Trail loops. After hiking these, follow the Bonner Trail to return to the Bluebird Hill Trail and finish the route.

12 Token Creek County Park

DISTANCE:	3.3 miles
ELEVATION GAIN:	100 feet
HIGH POINT:	930 feet
DIFFICULTY:	Easy to moderate
FITNESS:	Walkers, hikers, runners
FAMILY FRIENDLY:	Yes
DOG FRIENDLY:	Leashed dogs only, except in off-leash dog parks; Dane County Parks dog permit required.
AMENITIES:	Parking lot, restrooms, picnic shelters, interpretative info, dog parks, disc golf course, campground, playground
CONTACT/MAP:	Dane County Parks; map available online
GPS:	N 43°10'57.3" W 89°19'9.1"
BEFORE YOU GO:	Token Creek is one of the few county parks with a campground. The park has 37 sites (plus a group camp) that are reservable through Dane County Parks.

GETTING THERE

Driving: From Madison, follow Interstate 90 West to US Highway 51 (exit 32). Exit north and drive 0.3 mile to Williamsburg Way. Turn right immediately onto Token Creek Lane to enter Token Creek County Park. The trailhead for this route is across from picnic shelter 2.

I would call Token Creek County Park a hidden gem if its location wasn't so obvious. With Interstate 90 roaring along one side and houses and apartments within an easy walk or drive, this beautiful park is far from being a secret. Yet when you hike one of its trails through a sheltered oak forest or quiet marsh, the solitude is surprising. There are pros and cons to Token Creek County Park's location along Interstate 90. An obvious

A stand of pines at Token Creek County Park

drawback is the road noise that permeates its outer trail loops. Yet on the plus side, highway proximity also means this 400-acre park is easy to reach for most Madison-area hikers—not to mention interstate travelers and road-trippers who may need a place to stretch their legs. (Or exercise their pet; the county park includes dog parks for both large and small dogs.) Several miles of hiking trails—which become cross-country ski trails in winter—travel through the park, offering a look at woodlands, wetlands, and its namesake creek.

GET MOVING

This 3.3-mile loop begins at the cross-country ski trailhead, across the road from picnic shelter 2. Follow the trail south as it parallels the park road. To the right (west), Token Creek winds through the woods, widening into small marshy areas where you can hear frogs. Turn right (west) when you reach a mowed trail at the 0.2-mile mark, following it into the woods. For about a quarter mile, the trail passes through a verdant oak woodland, then climbs a small hill where you'll see the interstate through a gap in the trees.

At 0.5 mile, turn right at the T intersection. Just beyond this point, you'll reach the edge of the park's disc golf course. For the next 0.3 mile, the trail passes between the interstate and the disc golf course. While this is the loudest section of the hike, it also passes through some interesting woods with several species of wildflowers like wild blue phlox. (With the golf course on your left, be aware of the golfers and watch for flying discs.)

The trail turns east and heads away from the interstate around 0.8 mile, continuing through woods. At the 1-mile mark, you'll cross Token Creek Lane and pick up the trail again on the other side. Several trails converge at 1.1 miles; follow the trail that's second from the left to stay on route. At 1.3 mile, you'll reach the gate for the dog park. Cross in front of it to continue on the trail. For the next 0.3 mile, keep right at all trail junctures. When you reach the disc golf course again at 1.5 miles, turn right for a short detour around it. Turn right at the next intersection to rejoin the main trail.

From here, you'll hike through a few more meadows and woodlands before reaching a large area of wetlands. (Stay right at all junctions in this section.) The wetland sections of this trail can sometimes be flooded after heavy rains. Waterproof hiking boots are recommended. There is a short boardwalk at the 2.1-mile mark, and just beyond it is potentially the soggiest part of the trail. On one early summer hike, I found myself wading through ankle-deep water here. As you get closer to the campground, you'll cross two small bridges and catch glimpses of Token Creek on your right, a spring-fed tributary of the Yahara River that's being restored to brook trout habitat. At 2.4 miles, the trail enters the campground and intersects a paved path. Turn right to follow the paved path to the creek. A well-maintained boardwalk will take you on a slightly winding course along the creek. (Keep right when one section of boardwalk turns left into the campground at 2.6 miles.) The boardwalk ends at Token Creek Lane. Turn right onto the road and head toward the fishing pier ahead on the left. Starting at the fishing pier, follow the trail as it heads south along the creek. In early summer, there can be some beautiful wild roses along this stretch. Keep left for the next 0.2 mile until the trail ends at picnic shelter 1 and a playground. Turn right to reach the park's main road and walk south along it to return to your starting point.

MAKE IT SHORTER

For a 1.3-mile out-and-back hike that follows the creek, start at picnic shelter 1 and follow the trail in reverse along the creek. When you reach Token Creek Lane, turn right and look for the entrance to the boardwalk on your left. Hike along the boardwalk until it ends in the campground. Retrace your route to return to your starting point.

13 Governor's Island

DISTANCE:	1 mile
ELEVATION GAIN:	Minimal
HIGH POINT:	870 feet
DIFFICULTY:	Easy
FITNESS:	Walkers
FAMILY FRIENDLY:	Yes
DOG FRIENDLY:	Leashed dogs only
AMENITIES:	Parking lot
CONTACT/MAP:	Mendota Mental Health Institute; no map available
GPS:	N 43°7'37.4" W 89°24'0.1"
BEFORE YOU GO:	Portions of Governor's Island are open to duck hunting between September and December. Specific dates and areas can be verified with the Wisconsin Department of Natural Resources. Wear blaze orange and be aware of your surroundings if you hike during this time. If hiking with your dog, dress it in blaze orange too.

GETTING THERE

Public Transit: Madison Metro Route B stops along Troy Drive. From the intersection of Troy Drive and Main Drive (one of the Mendota Mental Health Institute's entrance roads), it's just over a half mile to Governor's Island. Head south on Main Drive for 0.3 mile, then turn left onto Governor's Island Parkway and follow it for about 0.3 mile to the parking lot at the north end of Governor's Island.

Driving: From State Highway 113 (Northport Drive) in north Madison, turn west onto Troy Drive. Continue for 1.3 miles and turn left (south) onto Main Drive. After 0.3 mile, turn left onto Cinder Lane, which becomes Governor's Island Parkway. Continue until the road ends in a parking lot.

Some of the best Lake Mendota views in Madison are seen from a little-known spot on its eastern shore: Governor's Island. Curiously, Governor's Island is not home to Wisconsin's governor, nor is it an island. It's a small public greenspace on the grounds of the Mendota Mental Health Institute, with a short, scenic trail. The place's name dates to the 1850s when Wisconsin's second-ever governor, Leonard J. Farwell, lived on the property. Back then, it really was an island; a causeway was built between the mainland and the island in the 1860s, turning it into the teardrop-shaped peninsula it is today. For a quick and easy hike with beautiful water views, try the trail here—especially around sunset when you can watch the western skies change color over the lake.

GET MOVING

This 1-mile route takes you around the perimeter of Governor's Island. Follow the trail south from the parking lot. The trailhead parking lot is on the causeway that was built more than 150 years ago. Once you reach the "island," turn right to follow its perimeter trail in a counterclockwise direction. Historical photos show that the center of the island was once cleared of trees, but the forest has since regrown. At the 0.2-mile mark, follow a short spur trail to the tip of a point.

A side trail at Governor's Island connects the main route to the lakeshore.

From here you can look north to Governor Nelson State Park on the opposite shore and the outflow of the Yahara River and Cherokee Marsh as they enter Lake Mendota. With lake access via a rocky beach, this is a popular fishing spot. Return to the main loop to continue the hike.

The south side of the island, which you'll reach around the half mile mark, is the best place to enjoy panoramic views of the UW–Madison lakefront and downtown. But with sandstone cliffs along the edge, there's limited access to the waterfront here. In the summer months, this is a popular stretch for paddlers and boaters to explore. At 0.6 mile, the trail turns north as it closes the main loop and returns to the parking lot.

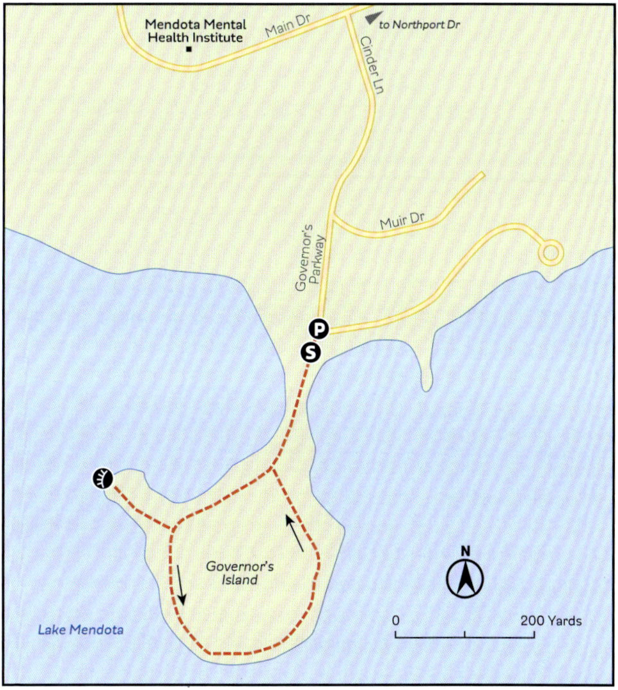

GO FARTHER

To add another half mile to your hike, don't stop once you return to the parking lot. Instead, hike along Governor's Island Parkway. It's a forested road that passes several burial mounds which are easier to see at a walking pace. When you reach Main Drive, turn around and return to the Governor's Island trailhead parking lot.

14 Warner Park

DISTANCE: 1.5 miles
ELEVATION GAIN: Minimal
HIGH POINT: 890 feet
DIFFICULTY: Easy
FITNESS: Walkers, runners
FAMILY FRIENDLY: Yes
DOG FRIENDLY: Leashed dogs only; off-leash dog park available
AMENITIES: Parking lot, restrooms, drinking water, interpretative info, accessible playground, picnic shelter, community recreation center, accessible fishing pier
CONTACT/MAP: City of Madison Parks Division; map available online
GPS: N 43°7'51.3" W 89°22'9.5"

GETTING THERE

Public Transit: Madison Metro Route B stops near the park's north entrance on Northport Drive, and Madison Metro Route D2 stops near the east entrance on North Sherman Avenue.

Driving: From downtown Madison, follow East Johnson Street north and continue when it becomes State Highway 113/Northport Drive. Follow WI-113 for 3 miles, then turn left (south) onto North Sherman Avenue. In a half mile, the park entrance will be on your right. Follow the park's road to the parking lot for the community recreation center.

Warner Park may be home to Madison's minor league baseball team, the Mallards, but it's also home to an abundance of plant and animal life—from actual mallards to a family of beavers. As Madison's second largest public park at 213 acres, Warner plays a crucial role in providing natural habitats in the midst of a city, including marsh, lagoon, prairie, and woodland. A paved path, nearly a mile long, curves through the property and along the lagoon, offering an accessible route for wheelchair users, strollers, and cyclists. There's also a small network of trails that crisscross the park's prairie and woods. Check the park's events calendar before you plan a visit, in order to participate in one of the park's many events—or to avoid crowds.

GET MOVING

This 1.5-mile route begins at Warner Park's Community Recreation Center. Just south of the community center, follow the paved path that heads west. At 0.1 mile, it intersects with the longer paved path that travels through the park. Turn left (south) onto this second path, which provides nice views of the lagoon and Castle Marsh at its center. Decades ago, this marsh was a spawning ground for northern pike, but years of development and runoff have unfortunately compromised this once thriving fish habitat. The trail crosses a small inlet, and at the 0.3-mile mark passes a large picnic shelter, an impossible-to-miss building with a roof made of rainbow-colored cylinders. From here, follow the paved path south over a second bridge and along the lagoon.

Continue south along the water where a paved connector path heads east to a parking lot. After crossing a creek at 0.5 mile and reaching a trail intersection, turn left (east) and look for a trail entering the woods on the right. Turn right (south) onto this trail. The next half mile through the wilder parts of the park is your best opportunity to see some of its wildlife residents. With its fresh water, prairie, and tree cover, Warner Park is a haven for an incredibly large and diverse population of birds. Local birders have recorded more than one hundred species nesting and traveling through the park, including bald eagles, great blue herons, American bitterns, and sandhill cranes. The park's list of mammal residents is equally impressive, with sightings of red foxes, white-tailed deer, short-tailed weasels, gray squirrels, and beavers.

Turn right at the 0.8-mile mark, then stay straight at the next intersection and cross the paved path. You'll rejoin it after you take a short trip through one of the park's prairies. Head right (north) when you reach a four-way trail intersection at 0.9

View across the Warner Park lagoon and Castle Marsh

mile. You'll pass a connector trail on your left before reaching another four-way trail intersection at the 1-mile mark. Turn right to return to the paved path. From here, you'll retrace your route north along the paved path to return to your starting point. You can either take a shortcut by using a connector path at the rainbow picnic shelter, or continue along your original route back to the north end of the parking lot.

MAKE IT SHORTER

For a shorter route that's wheelchair-accessible and stroller-friendly, travel the paved path that passes near the community recreation center. From this point, it's 0.6 mile (one way) to the north end of the park, or 0.7 mile to the south. Both sections will take you along the lagoon.

Next page: A connector links trails at Aldo Leopold Nature Center to Edna Taylor Conservation Park. (Trail 15)

SOUTHEAST

As the Yahara River flows southeast from downtown lakes Mendota and Monona, it eventually passes through the other lakes in the Yahara chain: Waubesa and Kegonsa. But first it travels through Capital Springs State Recreation Area, an environmental corridor with a patchwork of public lands. The parks and parcels in the 2,500-acre state recreation area include William G. Lunney Lake Farm County Park, Capital Springs State Park, Capital City Trail, Lower Yahara River Trail, and the Jenni & Kyle Preserve, among others. The hiking and biking trails at Lake Farm County Park and Capital Springs State Park—included in the following pages—wind through myriad landscapes, including sunny wildflower meadows and shaded Lake Waubesa shoreline. Further south, trails at Lake Kegonsa State Park travel through oak woods and prairie, with a side trail to the park's waterfront. But not all trails in the southeast area are lake-bound. There's plenty to see in the landscapes beyond—from a kid-friendly hike at Monona's Aldo Leopold Nature Center to a choose-your-own distance walk on the Glacial Drumlins State Trail.

15 Aldo Leopold Nature Center

DISTANCE:	1 mile
ELEVATION GAIN:	Minimal
HIGH POINT:	870 feet
DIFFICULTY:	Easy
FITNESS:	Walkers, hikers
FAMILY FRIENDLY:	Yes
DOG FRIENDLY:	Dogs not allowed
AMENITIES:	Nature center, parking lot, restrooms, educational programming and events, interpretative info
CONTACT/MAP:	Aldo Leopold Nature Center; map available online
GPS:	N 43°3'17.3" W 89°19'15.12"

GETTING THERE

Public Transit: Madison Metro Route 16 stops at the intersection of Pflaum Road and Monona Drive. From here, head south on Monona Drive for 0.6 mile. Turn left (east) on Femrite Drive. After 0.1 mile, turn left at the nature center entrance and follow the road to the parking lot and trailhead.
Driving: Take US Highway 12 to Monona Drive (exit 265). Head north on Monona Drive for 0.4 mile, then turn right onto Femrite Drive. After 0.1 mile, the entrance for the Aldo Leopold Nature Center will be on the left.

The Aldo Leopold Nature Center (ALNC)—named for celebrated conservationist and local ecological hero Aldo Leopold—is an environmental learning center tucked into a quiet Monona neighborhood, offering year-round programming for kids such as a nature preschool, day camps, and an after-school nature club. Beyond the nature center's walls is a network of walking trails through woods, prairie, and wetlands that are open to the public. With its focus on children, it's an ideal place to hike if you have little ones and school-age

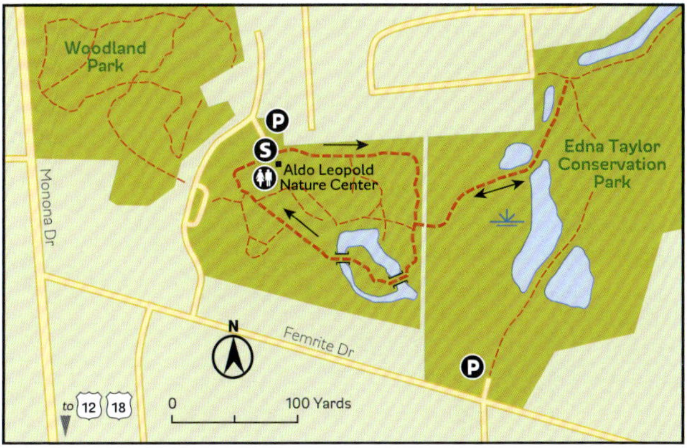

kids. The building's lobby, Nature Nook, and restrooms are also open to the public. You can even borrow a kid-friendly backpack from the front desk—full of fun nature gear—to take along on the trails. In addition to the nature center's property, visitors can also extend their hikes into one of the public parks on either side of the property: Woodland Park or Edna Taylor Conservation Park.

GET MOVING

This easy hike—it's just 1 mile long—includes a circuit through the ALNC's woods and wetlands, plus an out-and-back trek into the neighboring Edna Taylor Conservation Park. The trail starts on the east side of the nature center (that's left if you're facing the building's entrance). For the first several hundred feet, the path tunnels through a basswood forest where you'll sometimes see the happy signs of outdoor learning in action, like abandoned coats and lean-tos made of sticks.

Keep straight when another trail enters from the right around 0.1 mile. During the next several hundred yards, depending on the season and foliage, you might notice a trail or two veering to the left. To stay on route, always keep right.

(I speak from experience. A detour to the left can not only take you off the map but into a thorny mess.) Around the quarter-mile mark, turn left at the trail junction. This is where you'll begin the out-and-back section into Edna Taylor

The Aldo Leopold Nature Center has several kid-friendly trails.

Conservation Park. If you're unsure, there will be a sign on your left as the trail crosses into the park.

A short distance down this trail, the land opens to wetlands edged with prairie plants. In summer, look for purple-fringed wild bergamot and black-eyed Susans. At 0.3 mile, there's a pond hidden behind vegetation on the right and a small pond on the left with a wooden viewing platform. (The platform looked structurally unsound at the time of this writing. Use caution.) Just beyond this pond is a second, longer one. In midsummer, the ponds can be filled with pickerelweed, a beneficial native plant. Look for its glossy heart-shaped leaves and spike-like clusters of purple flowers. The trail intersection beyond the second pond is your turnaround point. Head back in the direction you came until you once again reach the trail junction at the border of the conservation park. Turn left (south) at this intersection to continue on the ALNC's trails.

Veer right at 0.7 mile and head toward the bridge that crosses onto a small island. Once there, you'll step into a quiet grove of tamarack trees—one of the most picturesque spots on the property. There's even a bench so you can linger here. The trail leaves the island on the opposite side, crossing another bridge. At this point, you'll have a clear view of the nature center across the prairie. It's about a quarter mile back to the starting point from here. Continue straight through the prairie to reach the nature center, then walk around the left side of the building to return to the main entrance and parking lot.

GO FARTHER

Woodland Park is a small, hilly greenspace distinguished by its striking oak savanna that's visible from Monona Drive. Today, 20 acres of the park are leased to the Aldo Leopold Nature Center, but the remaining 17 acres are a city park with its own set of short trails. Tack on a short loop through Woodland Park to the above route for a hike that's just over 1.5 miles.

16 Door Creek Park

DISTANCE:	2.1 miles
ELEVATION GAIN:	120 feet
HIGH POINT:	970 feet
DIFFICULTY:	Easy to moderate
FITNESS:	Walkers, hikers, trail runners
FAMILY FRIENDLY:	Yes
DOG FRIENDLY:	Leashed dogs only
AMENITIES:	Parking lot, restrooms, playground, cross country ski trails, tennis courts, pickleball courts, basketball courts, soccer field
CONTACT/MAP:	City of Madison Parks Division; map available online
GPS:	N 43°5'49.5" W 89°15'12.9"
BEFORE YOU GO:	The park's trails are open to snowshoeing and cross-country skiing in winter; skiers must purchase a permit.

GETTING THERE

Public Transit: Madison Metro Route D1 stops along Wyalusing Drive near its intersection with Littlemore Drive. Walk 0.4 mile east on Littlemore Drive to the park entrance.

Driving: From US Highway 12/18 in Madison, take exit 266 for US Highway 51 North. After 3.4 miles, turn right (east) on East Buckeye Road. Then after 2 miles, turn left on Sprecher Road. Drive 1.5 miles, then turn right on South Broad Creek Boulevard, followed by a left on Wyalusing Drive. Turn right on Littlemore Drive, and the park will be 0.4 mile ahead on the right.

Door Creek Park's namesake is a narrow 12-mile waterway that empties into Lake Kegonsa. Although a section of Door Creek flows through the park, it's mostly hidden from sight by an embankment and later, a dense wall of trees and shrubs. But creek view or not, this eastside park is full of other pleasant scenery like quiet woodlands and wild meadows, along

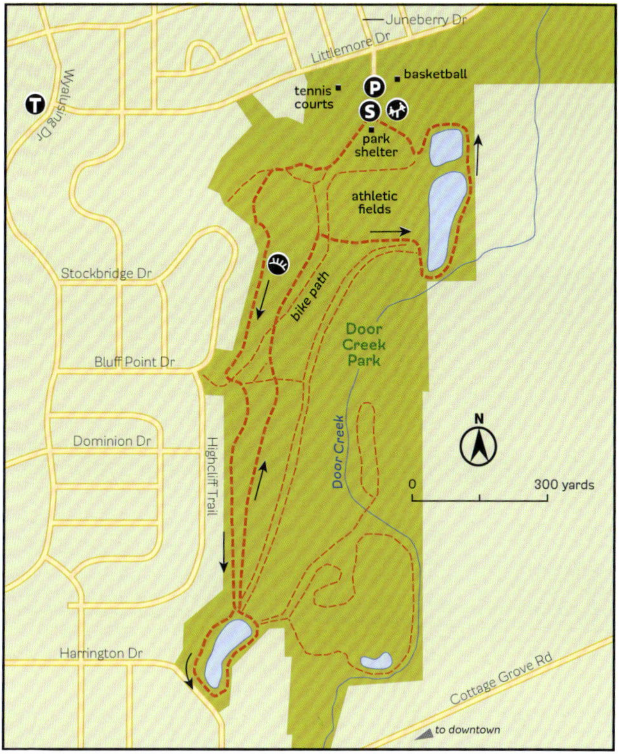

with recreational opportunities including tennis courts, athletic fields, a playground, and a few miles of hiking trails.

GET MOVING

Find the starting point for this route at the southwest corner of the parking lot, where a mowed trail leads into the prairie. Follow the trail right; you'll be hiking this route counterclockwise. At the edge of the woods, around 0.1 mile, veer right. Then stay to the right again at the next trail intersection. A couple hundred yards beyond this intersection, a trail branches off

Forest meets prairie at Door Creek Park

to the right. This path leads to private property, so be sure to keep left at this juncture to stay on route.

For the next quarter mile, the trail follows a ridgeline through a forest, with a neighborhood on one side and the occasional sweeping view to the prairie below. (There's an especially scenic vista around 0.3 mile, with wildflowers along the path and in the distance.) Several old apple trees grow along this route, so in late summer and early fall, look for fruit. Foraging is allowed in Dane County Parks. At 0.5 mile, watch for bikes and other trail users as you cross a paved path and continue to the trail on the opposite side.

After passing through another wooded section, the trail exits the trees beside a small pond. Walk counterclockwise around the pond, enjoying the shade of some large willows on the eastern edge. You'll return to the spot where you began your loop around the pond at the 1-mile mark. From here, instead of veering left and retracing your route back through the woods, turn right and follow the trail along the prairie. This trail parallels the first section of the hike but offers a different perspective and an up-close look at prairie plants.

Look for bikes and other trail users as you cross the path at the 1.4-mile mark; the trail continues on the opposite side as it enters the woods once more. At 1.5 miles, you'll exit the woods. Cross the paved path again and walk along the southern edge of the athletic fields to reach the trail on the far east side. At 1.6 miles, turn right at the T intersection and hike counterclockwise around two retention ponds. Door Creek flows just to the south of these ponds. Depending on the season, you may be able to glimpse it through the trees. Once you reach the northern end of the ponds, follow a paved path back to the parking lot and trailhead.

MAKE IT SHORTER

For a 1-mile hike on a paved path, begin at the parking lot. Follow the paved path for a half mile to the southern end of Door Creek Park; it'll pass between the park's prairie and woodland. The path is shared with cyclists and other trail users, so stay to the right. When you reach the southern edge of the park, turn around and retrace your route back to the parking lot.

17 Glacial Drumlin State Trail

DISTANCE: 5.6 miles
ELEVATION GAIN: 150 feet
HIGH POINT: 910 feet
DIFFICULTY: Easy to moderate
FITNESS: Walkers, hikers, runners
FAMILY FRIENDLY: Yes, and stroller-friendly, but be aware of bike traffic and road crossings.
DOG FRIENDLY: Leashed dogs allowed
AMENITIES: Parking lot, restrooms, drinking water, interpretative info
CONTACT/MAP: Wisconsin Department of Natural Resources; map available online
GPS: N 43°4'34.2" W 89°11'52.6"
BEFORE YOU GO: The Glacial Drumlin Trail is open to cyclists and pedestrians. Only cyclists need a trail pass. No pass or fee is required for pedestrians.

GETTING THERE

Driving: From Madison, head east on US Highway 12/18, crossing underneath Interstate 90. In 3.7 miles (after the interchange), take exit 272 for County Highway N. Drive 3.2 miles to downtown Cottage Grove; the entrance to the trailhead parking lot will be on the right.

The Glacial Drumlin State Trail crosses 52 miles of farmland and small towns as it heads east from Cottage Grove to Waukesha. Although it may be best known as a long-distance bike trail, it's also a pleasant walking route through grassland bird habitat—and provides a lesson in local geology. Drumlins, which give the trail its name, are the small, elongated hills dotting the landscape; some are easier to see than others. They were created by a retreating glacier at the end of the last ice age that left mixed

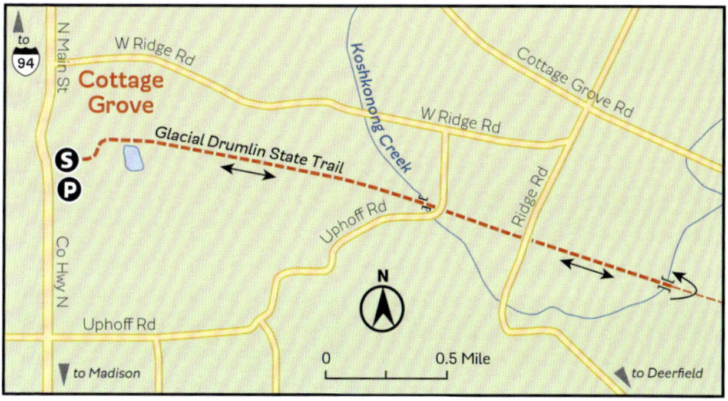

deposits of rock, gravel, and soil in its wake. Because of the drumlins' slopes and composition, the trees that grew on them were often spared from development, even as the land around them was tilled for farming. Look for these interesting formations along this trail and throughout southwestern Wisconsin.

GET MOVING

With more than 50 miles to choose from and many access points, a walk on the Glacial Drumlin State Trail is a choose-your-own-distance trek. For a longer hike on easy terrain that's not far from Madison, try this 5.6-mile out-and-back route. It begins in downtown Cottage Grove and includes two creek crossings. Begin at the Cottage Grove trailhead and follow the path east. The first mile or so is paved, but later turns to crushed limestone. As is the case with other "rails-to-trails" routes, it is mostly flat and level with a gentle grade.

At the 0.5-mile mark, you'll leave the town of Cottage Grove behind and head into the countryside. The next town on the trail is Deerfield, but at 6 miles away, you won't reach it on this hike. Despite having open fields on either side, for the most part the trail is lined with trees, their green canopy providing cool shade and bird habitat. The first few miles of

The Glacial Drumlin State Trail crosses Koshkonong Creek. (Photo courtesy of Manitou Media LLC)

the Glacial Drumlin Trail cross over the twisting Koshkonong Creek several times; the first is at 1.6 miles, where a bridge spans the creek. Koshkonong Creek flows for 54 miles from its headwaters near Sun Prairie to Lake Koshkonong, a reservoir first dammed in the 1930s. Although much of the creek's northern end was channelized and degraded over the years, a local effort to revitalize it is underway. Depending on when and where you go, it's possible you may see dredging efforts in progress as decades of harmful sediment and debris are removed.

A short distance beyond the creek crossing, the trail meets Uphoff Road. Watch for cars as you cross, and continue on the other side. From here the path keeps tunneling under trees until it crosses Ridge Road at the 2.1-mile mark. About a quarter mile beyond this junction, enter a marshy area as you approach the second creek crossing. This bridge over Koshkonong Creek is the turnaround point for this hike. One advantage of walking a rails-to-trails route is its easy navigation. To return to your starting point at the trailhead, simply turn around and walk back in the direction you came—no need to worry about taking a wrong turn.

GO FARTHER

There's no reason you need to turn around at the second creek crossing on this route. For a longer hike, just continue on the path. Or choose another section to hike along the 52-mile trail.

18 Capital Springs State Recreation Area

DISTANCE: 3.4 miles
ELEVATION GAIN: 70 feet
HIGH POINT: 870 feet
DIFFICULTY: Easy
FITNESS: Walkers, hikers
FAMILY FRIENDLY: Yes
DOG FRIENDLY: Leashed dogs only; Dane County Parks dog permit required
AMENITIES: Parking lot, restrooms, interpretative info, boat launch, fishing pier, campground, picnic shelters, disc golf course, dog park
CONTACT/MAP: Dane County Parks; map available online
GPS: N 43°1'35.9" W 89°19'57.6"

GETTING THERE

Public Transit: Madison Metro Route G has stops west of South Towne Drive/Raywood Lane and Moorland Road. At the intersection of South Towne Drive/Raywood Lane and Moorland Road, look for the Capital City Trail (a paved, multi-use path) running along the north side of Moorland Road. Follow the Capital City Trail 0.75 mile to the Lake Farm County Park entrance. It's quite a bit farther (another 0.75 mile) to the route described below, but you can easily access other hiking trails from the county park entrance.

Driving: From US Highway 12, take the exit for South Towne Drive and head south. After 0.8 mile, turn left (east) on Moorland Road, which shortly becomes Lake Farm Road. Proceed for another 0.8 mile and turn left (east) on Libby Road. Drive for 0.6 mile and turn left at the entrance for Lake Farm County Park. The trailhead for this route is the first parking lot on your right.

Each day, thousands of Madison commuters drive past one of the largest public green spaces in the area and never give it a second look. That's because the Beltline, the city's busiest highway, cuts across the sprawling northern wetlands of Capital Springs State Recreation Area. This collection of public lands—wetlands, lakeshore, prairie, savanna, and forest—covers more than 2,500 acres across eight distinct "units" linked by the multi-use Capital City Trail. Most of the recreation area's hiking trails are concentrated at William G. Lunney Lake Farm County Park and Capital Springs State Park on the eastern end, and pass through woodlands, prairies, and the Lake Waubesa shoreline. Although Capital Springs State Park was established in 2001, it is still under development and amenities are limited. Future plans include a rustic campground, amphitheater, and additional hiking trails.

Observation tower at William G. Lunney Lake Farm County Park

GET MOVING

Capital Springs State Recreation Area has several miles of hiking trails. For a loop that combines an open prairie with a wooded lakeside stroll, try this 3.4-mile route through Lake Farm County Park and Capital Springs State Park. With ample shade and lake breezes, add it to your "summer hikes" list. Find the trail at the northeast corner of the parking lot by the observation tower. After passing under the "Lake Farm Heritage Trail Head" sign, veer right at the fork, heading into the woods. At 0.2 mile, cross Libby Road (watch for traffic) and walk through the parking lot on the opposite side. Two trails enter the prairie here; follow the easternmost trail. You'll return on the other trail later.

While there are plans for future state park trails and camping in this area, for now it's a lush prairie full of wildflowers and grassland birds. When the trail reaches the woods at 0.5 mile, turn right at the intersection. Then turn left at the next intersection to follow a dead-end trail to the tip of Hog Island—depending on lake levels, the island is usually more of a marshy peninsula. After getting a look at Lake Waubesa, retrace your steps to the last intersection and turn left. You'll pass several giant oaks among the younger trees here. Keep left at the 1-mile mark when a trail branches right, and then again when a second trail heads right.

Head straight north at 1.1 miles, following a mowed trail back through the prairie. Keep your eyes open and your camera ready for native wildflowers like common milkweed, spiderwort, and white wild indigo. After a half mile, the trail returns to the parking lot on Libby Road. Find the trail again on the opposite side of the road and veer right at the fork, heading toward the boat launch and fishing pier parking lot. With restrooms, picnic tables, and lake views, this is an ideal spot to take a breather.

The trail enters the woods on the west side of the restroom building. For nearly a mile, this mostly shaded trail parallels Lake Waubesa, passing a public fishing pier and two picnic shelters. At 2.5 miles, you'll meet up with the busier Lower Yahara River Trail, a paved path that crosses a mile-long boardwalk. Rather than linking up with the Lower Yahara River Trail, however, follow the hiking trail as it makes a 180-degree turn, passing another path that veers right. For this final stretch, you'll hike through woodlands and a group camp. Keep left as you hike through the group camp. At the southern end of the group camp area at the 2.7-mile mark, follow the gravel road that heads right (west) to stay on route. After a couple hundred yards, turn left onto another gravel trail.

When you reach a pond at 3.1 miles, follow the trail that heads around its northern end. Despite the pond's small size, you may see wading birds such as great blue herons or egrets here. When you reach the southern end of the pond, keep left to follow the trail back to your starting point.

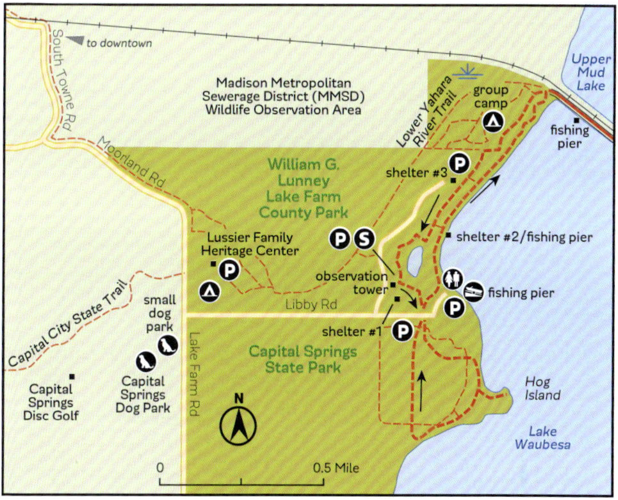

GO FARTHER

A detour on the Lower Yahara River Trail's boardwalk can add up to 2 miles to this hike's roundtrip distance for a total of 5.4 miles. Follow the route instructions until the 2.5-mile mark. Then turn right (east) onto the Lower Yahara River Trail. It's a mile-long walk along a boardwalk with views of the Yahara River and Lake Waubesa. When you reach McFarland's McDaniel Park, turn around and retrace your steps to continue the route.

19 Lake Kegonsa State Park

DISTANCE: 2.7 miles
ELEVATION GAIN: 100 feet
HIGH POINT: 910 feet
DIFFICULTY: Easy
FITNESS: Walkers, hikers, trail runners
FAMILY FRIENDLY: Yes
DOG FRIENDLY: Dogs are not allowed on the White Oak Nature Trail.
AMENITIES: Parking lot, restrooms, picnic tables, playground, campground, swimming beach, pet swim area
CONTACT/MAP: Lake Kegonsa State Park; map available online and on-site
GPS: N 42°58'48.8" W 89°14' 9.8"
BEFORE YOU GO: A state park vehicle admission sticker (daily or annual) is required year-round.

GETTING THERE

Driving: From US Highway 12/18 eastbound in Madison, take exit 266 for US Highway 51 South. After 1.2 miles, take the Siggelkow Road exit and turn left onto Siggelkow Road. Proceed for 2.7 miles to County Highway AB. Turn right onto County Highway AB, continue for 0.8 mile, then turn left

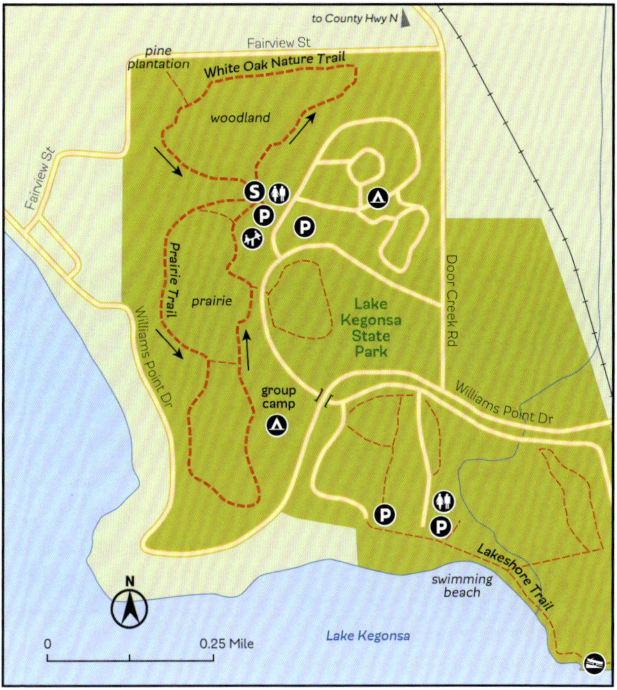

onto County Highway MN. After 0.7 mile, turn right onto Door Creek Road. In 2.5 miles, the state park entrance will be on your right. Once you enter the park, follow the signs for the White Oak Nature Trail parking lot.

People who don't venture beyond Madison's city limits may not realize that its downtown lakes—Mendota and Monona—belong to a chain of four lakes linked by the Yahara River. After flowing south through lakes Mendota, Monona, and Waubesa, the small but significant Yahara eventually reaches Lake Kegonsa, a 3,200-acre lake known for its fishing, particularly walleye and panfish like bluegill and perch. Lake Kegonsa

State Park stretches along its northeastern shore, offering camping and picnicking, along with a swimming beach, boat launch, and 5 miles of hiking trails.

GET MOVING

The trails at Lake Kegonsa State Park aren't especially long, but they offer a worthwhile, and somewhat rare, opportunity to experience natural shoreline and native habitat along one of the Yahara chain's lakes. Link together two of the park's loops for an easy and scenic hike.

From the parking lot, follow the signs for the White Oak Nature Trail. You'll pass a kiosk of pamphlets that describe points of interest along the way; borrow one for the hike. The numbered posts along this loop correspond to descriptions in the pamphlet. After the kiosk, keep right to hike the loop in a counterclockwise direction. The first quarter mile is a sloping dirt two-track that parallels the campground. In midsummer, the surrounding white oak woods are as leafy and emerald-bright as a rainforest. Although you can occasionally spot the campground through the trees, this trail still surprised me with its peace and solitude.

Around 0.3-mile, the trail turns nearly 180 degrees to the west and continues through the dense forest. Depending on the season, this moist forest habitat creates the perfect conditions for mushrooms. Take a closer look at the forest floor and decaying logs to see fungi like dyer's polypore and chicken of the woods. At 0.6 mile, follow a short spur trail to the right (northwest) to see a decades-old pine plantation. These towering red and white pines were planted in the late 1960s, around the time the state park was established. Pause here to listen for the calming whoosh of wind in the pine branches and smell the trees' refreshing scent. (This isn't just a pleasant perfume, either. Trees like pines release chemicals called

Prairie Trail at Lake Kegonsa State Park

phytoncides, which have been shown to reduce our stress levels and boost immunity.) Retrace your steps to return to the main loop and continue heading west.

HIKES BEYOND MADISON

For a day-long adventure or a weekend exploring the trails, head to one of these popular hiking destinations within an hour's drive from Madison.

- **Blue Mound State Park:** Blue Mound—the hill that gives the park its name—is the highest point in southern Wisconsin. Just twenty-five minutes west of Madison, this state park offers 20 miles of trails for hiking, mountain biking, and cross-country skiing. *Amenities: campground, restrooms, interpretative info, picnic areas, swimming pool and splash pad*
- **Devil's Lake State Park:** Less than an hour's drive from Madison, it's easy to see why this popular state park is packed on summer weekends: it has a clear glacier-carved lake surrounded by scenic bluffs and nearly 30 miles of hiking trails. *Amenities: campground, restrooms, interpretative info, picnic areas, boat rentals, swimming beaches, concessions*
- **Governor Dodge State Park:** As one of Wisconsin's largest state parks at 5,000 acres, Governor Dodge has an impressive 40 miles of trails through its forests and bluffs and around two lakes. *Amenities: campground, restrooms, interpretative info, picnic areas, boat rentals, swimming beaches, concessions*

In another 0.3 mile, you'll return to the beginning of the White Oak Nature Trail loop—but the hike doesn't end here. From this intersection, follow signs for the Prairie Trail, a wheelchair-accessible trail made from crushed stone. Keep right to hike this loop in a counterclockwise direction. At 1.1 miles, you'll get your first clear view of the picturesque prairie, hopefully with a wide blue sky above it. This small prairie is a haven for native plants like wild sunflowers and grassland bird species like bobolinks and horned larks. In late summer and early fall, late-blooming flowers like goldenrod buzz with bumblebees. Continue going straight when a connector trail enters at 1.4 miles. (This is a shortcut if you need a quick return to the trailhead.)

Around the 1.5-mile mark, the trail passes under trees again, providing cool shade during hot-weather hikes. From here, it makes a gradual turn north, passing the state park's group camps for about a quarter mile before emerging from the woods. Not long after, around 2.0 miles, a connector trail veers right. If you want a slightly longer hike, follow this trail as it crosses a road and loops around another prairie for about 0.4 mile. Otherwise, stay straight to continue the route. In another quarter mile, turn right to return to the trailhead parking lot.

GO FARTHER

For a short hike with lake views, start at the swimming beach parking lot and hike the paved Lakeshore Trail. It's a 1-mile hike roundtrip if you walk to the boat launch at the opposite end and back.

Next page: A shady trail in Elver Park (Trail 20)

SOUTHWEST

The abundance of hikes in southwest Madison and beyond is largely due to the Ice Age National Scenic Trail. National scenic trails are continuous routes of more than 100 miles that preserve areas of ecological, historical, and cultural significance. With fewer than a dozen such trails in the US, they are a storied group that includes the legendary Appalachian and Pacific Crest Trails. Wisconsin's Ice Age Trail was officially established by an act of Congress in 1980 and has been built and maintained by volunteers ever since. For 1,200 miles, the trail follows a moraine (a series of rocky, tree-covered ridges) and other unique geological features sculpted by the continent's last glacier as it retreated some 12,000 years ago. While thru hikers and backpackers camp along it, many people hike it in segments, a day hike at a time. Nine of the Ice Age Trail's one hundred-plus segments, marked by yellow blazes along the trail, are within a reasonable drive from Madison; seven of the nearest are included in this guidebook. And of course, the Ice Age Trail isn't the only route to walk on this side of the Madison metro area. There are also several county parks, a school forest, a few preserves, and the largest city park in Madison: Elver Park.

20 Elver Park

DISTANCE:	3.1 miles
ELEVATION GAIN:	300 feet
HIGH POINT:	1140 feet
DIFFICULTY:	Easy to moderate
FITNESS:	Hikers, walkers, trail runners
FAMILY FRIENDLY:	Yes
DOG FRIENDLY:	Leashed dogs only
AMENITIES:	Parking lot, restrooms, picnic shelters, playground, splash pad, disc golf course, athletic fields
CONTACT/MAP:	City of Madison Parks Division; map available online
GPS:	N 43°2'17.5" W 89°30' 9.9"
BEFORE YOU GO:	A portion of this route passes through the park's disc golf course, so yield to any golfers and keep an eye out for flying discs. In winter, avoid hiking on the park's groomed cross-country ski trails.

GETTING THERE

Public Transit: Madison Metro Route E has stops along McKenna Boulevard directly in front of the park.

Driving: From US Highway 12, take the exit for Gammon Road (exit 255) and turn left (south). After 1 mile, Gammon Road becomes McKenna Boulevard, and you'll see Elver Park on your right. To enter the parking lot, turn right at the traffic light.

At 250 acres, Elver Park is the largest city park in Madison. When I first visited it many years ago, I was surprised at how quickly the west side's hubbub and traffic gave way to forest and open fields. As development has continued beyond its boundaries, Elver Park remains a welcome haven for wildlife, plants, and people. It's also packed with year-round opportunities for outdoor recreation—from hiking trails, soccer fields, and a playground in the warmer months to lighted cross-country ski trails, sledding, and skating in the winter. No matter when you visit, keep an

eye (and ear) out for animal residents like great horned owls and white-tailed deer.

GET MOVING

Elver's hiking trails do double duty as popular ski trails once the snow flies, so the park has a large network of well-maintained trails to explore year-round. Try this 3.1-mile hike that takes you on a circuit through the park's quiet forests. Start at the main parking area near the playground and head southeast across (or around, if necessary) the athletic fields. At the park's eastern edge, a mowed trail leads into the prairie. Follow this trail as it makes a slow climb and turns south. (With busy McKenna Boulevard to your left, this will be the loudest section of the hike.) At 0.4 mile, continue straight when two consecutive trails branch right.

The trail reaches the disc golf course at 0.5 mile, where you'll see the cement slab tees for hole 10. Yield to any golfers and let them know you'll be walking through. For the next 0.3

mile, the route continues through the disc golf course, passing holes 10, 11, 12, and 13. A grove of old pines along hole 13 is especially scenic. (If you're up for a hike in winter, it's magical during a snowfall.) The trail leaves the disc golf course at 0.8 mile and descends through the woods in a few switchbacks. After rain or snow, this section can be especially slick. At the bottom, you'll exit the woods and see the main parking lot to the northeast. Turn left (west), following the trail through an open area and back into woods.

At 1.3 miles, the trail crosses a paved cul-de-sac. Follow the paved path that re-enters the park on your right; it heads downhill and over a wooden footbridge. At the T intersection, turn left. When you reach the end of the paved path, keep heading west on the mowed trail that leads to the woods. At 1.6 miles, stay left at the fork and follow the lower trail. In about a quarter mile, it turns sharply and heads north, where there is another fork; keep left. In spring, this section is full of woodland wildflowers—purple wild geraniums line the trail and spread across the forest floor. Look closer and you'll also

Peaceful pine forest at Elver Park

see jack-in-the-pulpit, mayapples, and violets. If you're hiking near sunset, listen for the calls of the great horned owls that frequent this part of the forest.

Around the 2-mile mark, there's an intersection of several trails. Take the one that's farthest left, then stay left for the next 0.3 mile as other trails branch off to the right. At 2.3 miles, the trail turns sharply, heading north, then northwest, along the park's border. Keep right as you encounter a couple of connector trails. When you reach a trail intersection at 2.6 miles, turn left and follow the trail through the woods until you reach a parking lot. From here, follow the park's road—or take a shortcut across the grass—to return to your starting point.

MAKE IT SHORTER

For a hike that takes half the time, follow the above route up to the 1.1-mile mark. When you exit the woods and can see the parking lot, take a shortcut across the field back to your starting point.

21 Ice Age Trail: Madison Segment

DISTANCE:	3.2 miles one way
ELEVATION GAIN:	250 feet
HIGH POINT:	1160 feet
DIFFICULTY:	Easy to moderate
FITNESS:	Walkers, hikers, trail runners
FAMILY FRIENDLY:	Yes
DOG FRIENDLY:	Dogs are not allowed on the trail section between County Highway M and Woods Road. On the rest of the route, leashed dogs are allowed.
AMENITIES:	Parking lot, restrooms (seasonal), interpretative info
CONTACT/MAP:	Ice Age Trail Alliance; map available online and on-site
GPS:	N 43°0'55.3" W 89°31'12.0"

GETTING THERE

Public Transit: Madison Metro Route E has stops near Muir Field Road and County Highway PD/McKee Road. From the intersection of Muir Field and McKee, walk west along McKee for 0.4 mile to reach the trailhead parking lot.

Driving: From County Highway M/South Pleasant View Road in Madison, turn east onto County Highway PD/McKee Road. After 0.8 mile, the entrance to the trailhead parking lot will be on your right. University Ridge Golf Course is an alternative start or end point for this hike. Hikers are allowed to park in the lower parking area when the golf course is open.

The suburban Madison segment of the Ice Age Trail—an easy 3.2-mile journey through woods, neighborhoods, and a golf course—is a good way to experience a long-distance hiking trail without venturing too far from home or into the wilderness. Most of the IAT's sections (like this one) are not loops, however, and must be hiked from end-to-end. That means if you want to hike the entire Madison segment, you need to catch a ride, arrange a shuttle with your fellow hikers (parking a car at either end), or commit to a 6.4-mile hike. The Ice Age Trail Alliance designates Woods Road as the Madison segment's starting point and County Highway PD (McKee

Road) as its endpoint. But for people who are not thru-hiking the trail, I recommend hiking this segment in reverse, beginning at the McKee Road trailhead, since there is no parking lot on Woods Road, nor a shoulder where cars can safely pull off.

GET MOVING

Follow the paved bike path at the south end of the trailhead parking lot on McKee Road. Turn right (west) and follow the bike path over the pedestrian bridge. After crossing the bridge, turn left (west) and look for the yellow blazes that mark the Ice Age Trail. After crossing a paved connector path twice, follow the packed dirt hiking trail as it heads north. It parallels the bike path for a half mile as it meanders through woods along the edge of a neighborhood.

The hiking trail joins the bike path just before it crosses Raymond Road. Watch for traffic as you cross, then hike across the wooden bridge that spans a seasonal creek. Just beyond the bridge, look for the Ice Age Trail as it enters the woods on the left (west) side of the bike path. Despite its nearness to a neighborhood and busy bike path, this wooded section feels like a haven hidden in plain sight. If you hike this trail near sunset, you may hear one of the owls or coyotes that make their home here.

Around the 1-mile mark, the woods give way to prairie as the trail continues alongside Flagstone Park toward South Pleasant View Road. Turn left when the hiking trail intersects with the bike path, and follow it through the tunnel under South Pleasant View Road. Once you're through the tunnel, instead of following the bike path to the right (north), take the dirt hiking trail south as it crosses a small covered bridge. Stay straight when a service road turns right. When you reach the parking lot for the O. J. Noer Turfgrass Facility, veer right and follow the paved path on the other side of the parking lot. At 1.5 miles, follow the trail as it heads right (west) off the paved path.

At 1.6 miles, you'll enter a forest and cross a bridge over a narrow gully. From this point on, the trail winds through University Ridge Golf Course. At 2.1 miles, the trail meets the golf cart path. Watching for carts, turn left (west) onto the paved path. Walk along it for about a hundred yards, then follow the hiking trail heading into the grass on the left side of the path. You'll cross the golf cart path twice more before the trail turns north and begins a slow and steady climb. Once you gain enough elevation, turn around for a sweeping view of the surrounding landscape and Verona beyond.

At 2.5 miles, the hiking trail intersects a paved path and a gravel service road. Stay straight (north) to hike along the paved path. At the entrance to the golf cart parking lot, veer left to cross the golf course's driveway (watch for traffic). The hiking trail continues on the other side. (Alternatively, you could also stop at the University Ridge clubhouse for water, snacks, or restrooms. It's open to hikers and the public.) At 2.7 miles,

The Ice Age Trail's Madison segment passes through University Ridge Golf Course.

you'll enter the final, and longest, stretch of woods in the route's northern end. Although it's just a few steps away from the golf course, the trail here has a secluded feel, thanks to a leafy understory. The end of the Madison segment, on Woods Road, is marked by a wooden gate and information kiosk. If you're hiking this route as an out-and-back, this is your turnaround point.

MAKE IT SHORTER

For a shorter hike that doesn't require shuttling, catch the trail at the University Ridge Golf Course's lower parking lot and head north. From here, it's a 1.4-mile roundtrip hike to Woods Road and back, through a pretty woodland.

22 Madison School Forest

DISTANCE:	3.9 miles
ELEVATION GAIN:	380 feet
HIGH POINT:	1100 feet
DIFFICULTY:	Moderate
FITNESS:	Hikers
FAMILY FRIENDLY:	Yes; some steep and narrow sections may be difficult for younger children.
DOG FRIENDLY:	Dogs not allowed
AMENITIES:	Parking lot, restrooms (seasonal)
CONTACT/MAP:	Madison Metropolitan School District and Wisconsin Department of Natural Resources; map at trailhead
GPS:	N 42°56'42.6", W 89°35'18.8"

GETTING THERE

Driving: Head south on US Highway 151 from Madison. Exit on State Highway 69 in Verona and head south for 1.2 miles. Turn right (west) on Riverside Road and follow it for 2 miles, then turn left (south) on Fritz Road. After 1 mile, the trailhead with a gravel parking lot will be on the left.

With its rich biodiversity and microclimates like shadowy ravines and fern-covered cliff faces, the Madison School Forest offers opportunities for outdoor learning—and several miles of hiking trails. (Snowy winter walks are especially beautiful here.) The school forest got its start in the 1950s when two local men envisioned an outdoor classroom for students, a forest owned by the school district just south of Verona. In the years since, the Madison School Forest—which now includes Olson Oak Woods State Natural Area, two prairies, and a group camp—has grown to just over 300 acres and is a hub of environmental education. The trails are free and open to the public, but keep a map handy. It's easy to end up on the wrong trail, especially in summer when trails can become overgrown and signage hard to see. Also, the trails are usually not busy, but you may encounter school field trips if hiking on weekdays during the school year.

GET MOVING

To take in (almost) the entire Madison School Forest property, hike a circuitous 3.9-mile route consisting of three loops, which starts at the main trailhead on Fritz Road. Take the trail that begins at the south end of the parking lot, and follow the signs for the Cliff Edge Trail. At 0.1 mile, turn right (south). You'll hike back to this point after making a loop through the first prairie. (If you're hiking with young children and prefer to avoid the steepest and narrowest parts of this hike, you can continue straight here, rather than hiking the Cliff Edge Trail loop.) When you reach a fork at 0.3 mile, turn right to follow the trail through the open meadow. This sheltered stretch, with trees on all sides, is prime songbird habitat. Although the on-site map indicates otherwise, the trail ends at Fritz Road at the 0.5-mile mark instead of linking up with the Cliff Edge Trail. Watch for traffic and turn left onto Fritz Road. Less than 100 yards down the road, follow the Cliff Edge Trail as it enters the woods on the left (east) side of the road.

The next quarter mile is the steepest part of the hike as the trail climbs above the meadow. At the 1-mile mark, veer right at the trail fork and retrace your steps to where the Cliff Edge Trail intersects with the Prairie Relic Trail. Turn right (east) onto the Prairie Relic Trail. After heading down into a gully, you'll cross a shallow seasonal creek. Turn right (south) when a trail branches off at 1.3 miles. This connector trail is lined with wild geraniums in the spring and leads to a loop around a large restored prairie. When you reach the prairie, turn right and follow the trail around its perimeter. Along the way, you'll see beehives, wildflowers, and some buildings from the land's former use as a farm.

At the 2.4-mile mark, turn right (north) toward the woods, retrace your steps back to where this trail intersects the Wilderness Trail, and turn right (east). At 3.2 miles, you'll reach a large shelter that's used as an outdoor classroom during field trips and school programs. Several trails converge at this

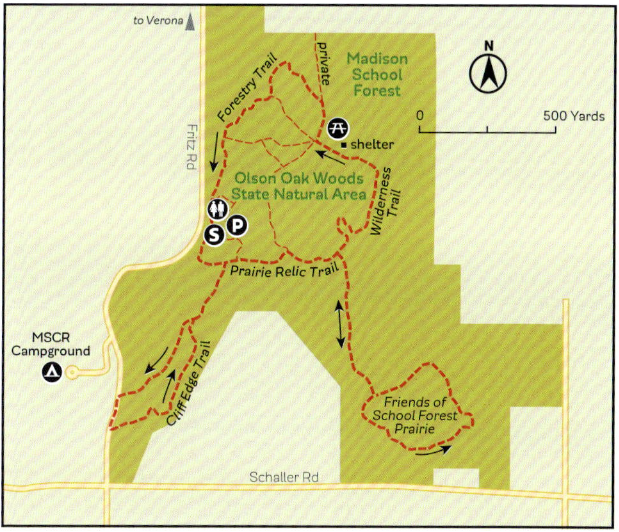

grassy clearing in the woods; to continue the route, turn right (north) onto the Old Wagon Trail. At 3.3 miles, look left (west) to see the Forestry Trail, a narrow dirt trail leading deeper into the woods. Follow this trail to stay on route. Although the Old Wagon Trail continues north, from this point on, it's private and not open to hikers.

The Forestry Trail heads briefly toward the northwest before turning back south for the final stretch. The forest here is full of long-lived hardwoods like white, red, and black oak, along with hickory and elm—there are even some trees here that date back to the 1750s. It's no wonder that around forty bird species make their home in this woodland habitat. Keep right at all trail junctions for the final half mile; the Forestry Trail will end at the Fritz Road trailhead where you started.

The Madison School Forest property includes more than 300 acres of woods and prairie.

MAKE IT SHORTER

For a shorter, forest-only hike, follow the route above, but don't hike the two smaller prairie loops or their connector trails. The total trip distance will be about 1.5 miles.

23 Scheidegger Forest

DISTANCE: 1.1 miles
ELEVATION GAIN: 120 feet
HIGH POINT: 1050 feet
DIFFICULTY: Easy
FITNESS: Walkers, hikers, trail runners
FAMILY FRIENDLY: Yes
DOG FRIENDLY: Leashed dogs only; Dane County Parks dog permit required.
AMENITIES: Parking lot, picnic shelter, overnight group camp, benches, restrooms, interpretative info
CONTACT/MAP: Dane County Parks; map available online
GPS: N 42°57'13.8" W 89°31'21.2"
BEFORE YOU GO: This county forest is open to bow-hunting during the fall and winter deer and turkey seasons (mid-September–early January). Wear blaze orange and be aware of your surroundings if you hike during this time. If hiking with your dog, keep it leashed and dress it in blaze orange too.

GETTING THERE

Driving: From Verona, head south on County Highway PB. Turn right (west) on Sunset Drive. After 0.6 mile, turn right (north) on Range Trail and continue for another 0.25 mile. The entrance and parking lot for Scheidegger Forest is on the right.

Scheidegger Forest may be one of Dane County's smallest public lands, but it has a wooded 1.1-mile loop that's a peaceful and pretty place to hike, especially in the summer. Its short distance and gentle terrain make it an ideal route for kids or novice hikers. Scheidegger's 80 acres were most recently home to a shooting range for the county sheriff's department, but since 2010, it's been a county forest and the site of ongoing restoration work. Today most of the landscape is a managed forest of oaks and hickories. (The shelter, restroom, and information kiosk were all built from timber harvested from the site.) In the warmer months, enjoy the park's welcome shade and woodland wildflowers. Then come back for fall color—and winter quiet after the snow falls. Winter trails here are not groomed but are open to cross-country skiing and snowshoeing.

GET MOVING

Scheidegger Forest's only trail begins and ends at the parking lot, and you can hike it in either direction. For this route, begin

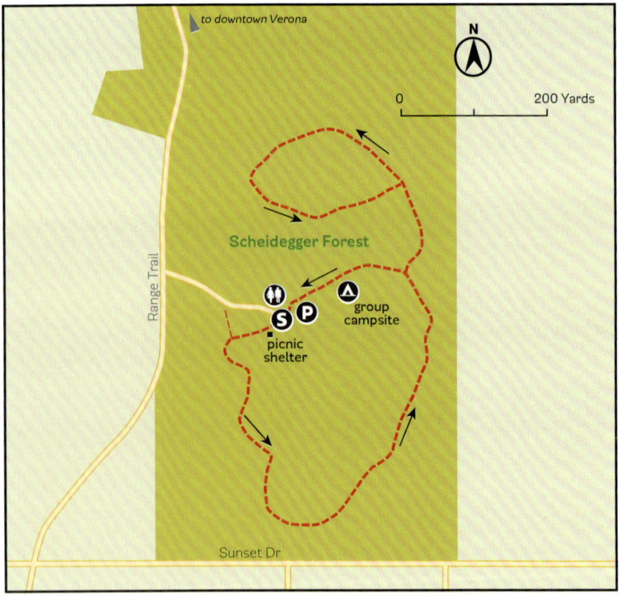

the 1.1-mile loop at the southwest end of the parking lot and travel counterclockwise. To start, you'll cross a meadow on your way up to the woods. Keep an eye out for grassland birds like goldfinches during the summer and fall when plants are in bloom.

At 0.1 mile, enter the forest and continue a moderate climb. The forest is the reason for the park's existence. The trees here are a mix of oaks (bur, red, white, and black), along with black walnut, shagbark hickory, red maple, and aspen. The master plan for the park involves restoring the oak savanna and woodland through invasive species removal and sustainable timber harvest. Some tree species, such as black walnut, are selectively harvested by the county, and the revenue from the timber is used for the park's management.

The trail makes a wide U-turn through the forest and begins heading north. A neighborhood borders the park's eastern edge, and at around 0.4 mile, you'll see some houses through the trees. Just beyond, at the half-mile mark, you'll reach a trail intersection. Head straight to continue the route—or if need be, turn left to head back to the parking lot. Not long after that intersection, you'll reach another one. This is the beginning—and end—of the trail's northernmost loop. Stay right to hike the loop counterclockwise; you'll be returning on the left. The northern part of the hike is similar to the southern section, with tall trees and lots of songbird chatter. On past hikes, I've heard and seen great horned owls in this part of the forest. If you're hiking near sunset, you just might hear one, or its smaller relative, the barred owl. When the trail loops back to the intersection, keep right. Then, when you reach the next intersection at 0.9 mile, turn right again. From here, it's a quick downhill walk back to the parking lot. On the way, you'll pass an overnight group campsite that's reservable through the county.

The trail at Scheidegger Forest begins in a wildflower meadow.

MAKE IT SHORTER

If factors like weather or tired kids necessitate an even shorter hike, you can easily keep your hike to a half mile. Just begin at the far east side of the parking lot (beyond the group campsite). Once you reach the trail intersection in the woods, turn left for a 0.4-mile loop, or turn right for one that's slightly longer than that.

24 Valley View Preserve

DISTANCE:	3.8 miles
ELEVATION GAIN:	530 feet
HIGH POINT:	1200 feet
DIFFICULTY:	Easy to moderate
FITNESS:	Walkers, hikers
FAMILY FRIENDLY:	Yes
DOG FRIENDLY:	Leashed dogs only
AMENITIES:	Parking lot, interpretive info
CONTACT/MAP:	Ice Age Trail Alliance; map available online and on-site
GPS:	N 43°2'22.1" W 89°34'57.2"
BEFORE YOU GO:	This route includes part of the national scenic Ice Age Trail, but no trail pass or fee is required; parking is also free at the trailhead. This hike borders private land and passes through a few residential neighborhoods, so be sure to stay on the trail.

GETTING THERE

Driving: From South Pleasant View Road on Madison's far west side, turn west onto Midtown Road. After 4.3 miles, turn right (north) onto Mound View Road. Continue for about a half mile and turn left (west) at Moraine Ridge. The first right leads to a small parking lot and trail access.

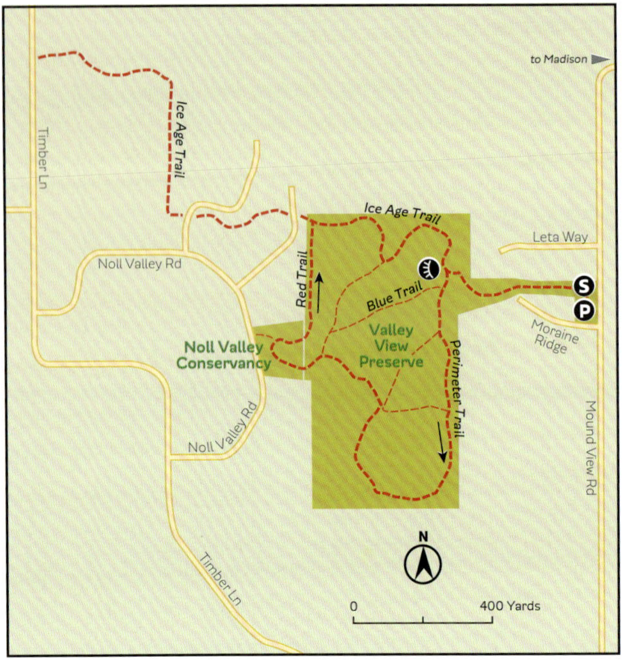

Sometimes there are beautiful places to explore in our own neighborhoods that we somehow fail to see. I've lived within a few miles of Valley View Preserve for more than a decade and only discovered it while writing this hiking guide. My family and I stumbled into it on a golden autumn evening while hiking a segment of the Ice Age Trail. With winding trails, long-lived trees, and open vistas across a prairie, it's especially magical the hour or two before sunset. The preserve is about 14 acres, but the quiet atmosphere and long views make it feel much larger.

GET MOVING

For a relatively easy hike (there are some steeper sections) that's just under 4 miles, I recommend combining a loop through the preserve with a section of the Valley View segment of the Ice Age Trail. From the trailhead parking lot on Moraine Ridge, follow the Ice Age Trail through the meadow—in late summer and fall, it's colorful with New England asters and other blooms. For the first quarter mile, you'll pass through a neighborhood before heading downhill into the woods. The trail narrows here as it passes under the trees and crosses a gully on a wooden footbridge. Despite the leafy canopy and dense understory, the trail's high vantage point provides glimpses through the trees of the grander view to come.

As you exit the woods at 0.3 mile, you'll reach a T intersection. Instead of taking a right and continuing on the Ice Age Trail, turn left to follow the Perimeter Trail into Valley View Preserve. Once a horse farm, the 14-acre preserve—now managed by the Ice Age Trail Alliance—has been a decades-long ecological restoration project for a group of volunteers. As you'll see en route, the restoration work, including prescribed burns and invasive species removal, is still happening. As you head south into the preserve, several shortcuts veer right. Keep left to stay on the preserve's outermost loop.

The trail takes an undulating course through open woods, restored prairie, and former horse pasture. Despite the neighborhoods just beyond the preserve's borders, the place is blissfully quiet except for birdsong. There are interpretive signs along the way, but most are a bit weather-beaten and difficult to read. Around 0.8 mile, the trail gradually turns and heads north, taking a downhill track through a lovely forest of bur oaks and hickories, followed by more prairie. You'll pass a bench or two along the way in case you need a breather or want to soak up the silence. At 1 mile, turn left at a four-way intersection. Keep left until the preserve trail links up with the Ice Age Trail at 1.6 miles, then turn left to follow the Ice Age Trail.

At this point, you'll exit the woods, hike along a wooden fence, and cross the end of a private driveway. The trail continues on the other side, re-entering woods and beginning a short, steep climb. At 2.8 miles, the trail once again crosses the end of a driveway, then takes a sharp right (north) turn through woods. Follow the trail for another half mile until you reach Timber Lane. This is your turnaround point and the end of the Ice Age Trail's Valley View segment. Head back the way you came, retracing your steps until you reach the trail intersection at 3.1 miles. This time, rather than taking a right and hiking through the preserve, continue straight on the Ice Age Trail. You'll continue to climb uphill all the way back to your starting point, and the views get better as you go. At 3.4 miles, there's a nice bench that offers a stunning view of the prairie and faraway Blue Mound. It's an incredible place to watch the sunset. From here, stay left and retrace your route for another 0.4 mile back to the trailhead parking lot.

Late summer asters along the Ice Age Trail's Valley View segment

GO FARTHER

This hike includes most of the Ice Age Trail's Valley View segment. If you'd like to hike the entire section, you can begin this hike at the southern end of the segment on Midtown Road. There's street parking only here, and the route requires walking along a couple of roads. If you do an out-and-back hike from Midtown Road, the total mileage—including the preserve loop—is 4.5 miles. I'd only recommend tacking on this southern section if you're attempting to hike the Ice Age Trail segment by segment.

25 Badger Prairie County Park

DISTANCE: 2.3 miles
ELEVATION GAIN: 140 feet
HIGH POINT: 1050 feet
DIFFICULTY: Easy
FITNESS: Walkers, hikers, trail runners
FAMILY FRIENDLY: Yes
DOG FRIENDLY: Leashed dogs only; Dane County Parks dog permit required.
AMENITIES: Parking lot, picnic shelter, restrooms, playground, dog park, mountain bike trails, aeromodelling field
CONTACT/MAP: Dane County Parks; map available online
GPS: N 42°59'56.8" W 89°30'50.0"
BEFORE YOU GO: Most hiking trails at this park are also open to mountain bikes, so be aware of other trail users and share the trail.

GETTING THERE

Public Transit: Madison Metro Route 75 stops at the Verona Park & Ride on East Verona Avenue. From here, you can follow the paved bike path north under East Verona Avenue and into the county park.

Driving: From Madison, head south on US Highway 18/151 toward Verona. Take exit 81 for East Verona Avenue and turn right immediately onto Maple Grove Drive. The first left after this intersection is the entrance for Badger Prairie County Park. After entering the park, follow the main road to the parking lot and trailhead beside the dog park.

In southern Wisconsin, it can be easy to take prairie habitat for granted, with its shoulder-high grasses and colorful wildflowers. After all, most hikes in this guide pass through at least some prairie landscape. But prairies are a familiar sight here only because of people who took the initiative to either save or restore them. Badger Prairie County Park, a 350-acre park between the ever-expanding cities of Verona and Madison, is an example of both preservation and restoration. Badger Prairie Soccer Fields leases the park's northwestern section—and a former landfill site is now an airfield for model plane enthusiasts—but the rest is a mix of restored prairie, fallow grassland, and woods with a network of hiking and mountain bike trails.

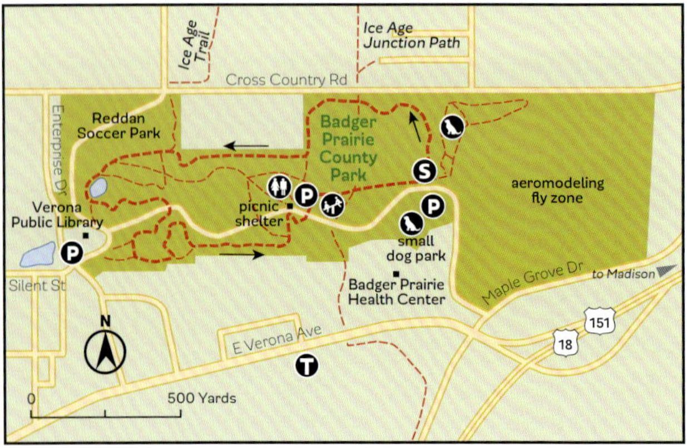

GET MOVING

A prairie's best season is mid- to late summer when it reaches its full height and is crowded with blooms, like sprays of sunflowers and purple tufts of field thistle. For an easy 2.3-mile hike around the park's grassland and prairie flowers, begin at the wooden "Mountain Bike Trailhead" sign just beyond the north edge of the parking lot. (Hikers and mountain bikers share many of the same trails here, but there isn't usually much bike traffic.)

Follow the trail north from the trailhead. You'll notice a loud buzz for the first quarter mile that will fade as you head deeper into the park; the noise comes from the generators at the former landfill site within the park (now a field for model airplanes). As an interesting ecological sidenote, the generators use biogas from the underground trash to generate electricity, providing nearly all the electricity needs for the neighboring Badger Prairie Health Center. When you reach a trail juncture at 0.1 mile, veer left (west). The sweeping land on the left (south) is fallow grassland. Although it hasn't been planted with native species like the park's restored prairie, this land is important habitat for ground-nesting birds.

At 0.3 mile, watch for bicyclists and other trail users as you cross the paved Ice Age Junction Path and continue toward the tree line up ahead. At 0.5 mile, turn right (west) at the trail intersection and begin a steady climb. You'll soon notice a change in the landscape as the muted hues of the grassland give way to the brighter greens and blooms of the restored prairie. In late summer, it is a kaleidoscope of yellow flowers, including goldenrod, sunflowers, and gangly compass plants. Late summer is also the ideal time to forage for plums on this route; several wild plum trees grow along the forest edge on the right (north) side of the trail.

Over the next 0.3 mile, continue straight as a few side trails intersect on the left and right. At 0.8 mile, the trail enters a section of Reddan Soccer Park and skirts its southern edge before turning south and heading back into the prairie. Keep right when the trail splits here, and you'll soon reach a pretty little pond, the park's only water feature. Follow the trail counterclockwise around the pond. You'll pass a spur trail on the right that leads to the Verona Public Library, a prairie-style building with large windows that overlook the park. As you leave the pond behind, the trail climbs toward the east, offering beautiful views of the prairie. Depending on the season, you might see wildflowers like the aptly named bottle gentian—with its blue clusters of bottle-shaped flowers—or purple coneflowers, a favorite of goldfinches and butterflies.

Watch for cars as you cross the park's interior road at the 1.2-mile mark, then continue hiking through the prairie. Keep left at the next trail junction, and hike along a small aspen grove. At 1.4 miles, turn left at the T intersection. You can take a shortcut at 1.5 miles by continuing straight, or turn left for the recommended (and more scenic) route. The latter takes you on an additional short loop through the prairie. At 1.7 miles, turn left and follow the trail as it parallels

The Verona Public Library sits at the edge of Badger Prairie County Park.

the park road. Stay right at all junctions for the next 0.2 mile until you reach the road and the picnic area parking lot. Cut through the parking lot to reach the trail along its eastern edge. At the next trail intersection, turn right. From here it's a short walk through the park's grasslands to return to the trailhead where you started.

MAKE IT SHORTER

For a short hike that's good for young children, start at the Verona Public Library parking lot. A trail (with two entrances) takes you into the county park's prairie just north of the library. A very short hike will take you to the small pond. Otherwise, walk an out-and-back route as far or as short as you'd like. (And as an added bonus, the Verona Public Library has an excellent children's section for some post-hike reading and play.)

26 Ice Age Trail: Verona Segment North

DISTANCE: 3.7 miles
ELEVATION GAIN: 320 feet
HIGH POINT: 1140 feet
DIFFICULTY: Easy to moderate
FITNESS: Walkers, hikers, trail runners
FAMILY FRIENDLY: Yes, although the distance is more suited to older children.
DOG FRIENDLY: Leashed dogs only
AMENITIES: Parking lot, restrooms (seasonal), interpretative info
CONTACT/MAP: Ice Age Trail Alliance; map available online and on-site
GPS: N 43°0'55.3" W 89°31'12.0"
BEFORE YOU GO: The trail section that passes through Badger Prairie County Park intersects with several mountain bike trails, so be aware of bikes and other trail users.

GETTING THERE

Public Transit: Madison Metro Route E has stops near Muir Field Road and County Highway PD/McKee Road. From the intersection of Muir Field and McKee roads, walk west along McKee for 0.4 mile to reach the trailhead parking lot.

Driving: From County Highway M/South Pleasant View Road in Madison, turn east onto County Highway PD/McKee Road. After 0.8 mile, the entrance to the trailhead parking lot will be on your right.

The fastest way through the heart of Verona is County Highway M. But there's a slower, nearly hidden journey running parallel that you can take on foot. The Ice Age Trail's Verona segment begins at the city's northern edge and traverses natural areas and traverses natural areas and neighborhoods for more than six miles before ending at Prairie Moraine County Park. The trail passes prairie and creek habitat, as well as regular reminders of its suburban setting—a public library, soccer park, and several busy thoroughfares. Because of its length (a roundtrip hike is more than 12 miles), I've divided the Verona segment into three smaller out-and-back hikes with easy-to-access trailheads. This first hike covers the segment's northern section: a roundtrip journey of 3.7 miles that begins and ends at the McKee Road trailhead, with its turnaround point at Badger Prairie County Park. Grasslands and open skies are the defining features of the hike, as it begins and ends in a wildflower-flocked prairie.

GET MOVING

This out-and-back hike begins at the south end of the trailhead parking lot. Cross the paved Ice Age Junction Trail, look for the "Ice Age Trail Access" sign, and follow the trail as it heads into the prairie. At the first trail intersection, turn left (south), following the yellow blazes for the Ice Age Trail. Stop and enjoy the panoramic view when you reach the route's highest point at 0.3 mile. Looking south, you can see all the way to Prairie Moraine County Park, the official end of the Verona

Heading south to Verona on the Ice Age Trail

segment. As the trail descends nearly 1.5 miles to your turnaround point, you'll enjoy a gently sloping trail most of the way.

At 0.5 mile, head straight (south) at the trail intersection. This is the only forest on the route, so take advantage of the brief shade if it's a hot day. After exiting the woods, you'll reach an intersection of several trails around the 0.7-mile mark. Continue heading south and follow the yellow blazes to stay on the Ice Age Trail. For the next half mile, stay straight at all junctions as the route travels through meadows that lie to the east of Reddan Soccer Park. In summer and fall, look for wildflowers like goldenrod and asters. The trail abruptly ends at the edge of the meadow at the 1.2-mile mark. To pick it up again, head west toward the soccer park entrance. Watch for traffic and turn left (south), using the crosswalk to reach the other side of Cross Country Road. Continue to head south, and in a few hundred feet you'll see the Ice Age Trail—a mowed trail at this point—veer left into the prairie.

The next part of the hike passes through Badger Prairie County Park. The park has several loops of hiking and mountain bike trails in addition to the Ice Age Trail, so pay close attention to the map and route description. As you hike into the prairie, stay straight at the first two trail junctions. At 1.5 miles, turn left (south), then left (east) again as you gradually climb to the top of a hill. Continue heading straight (east) at the next trail intersection. At 1.6 miles, you'll reach an overlook with a bench.

Beyond this point, the trail curves left around a hill and merges with a gravel service road. Stay straight (southeast) at the next trail intersection, then turn left (east) at 1.7 miles. Turn right (south) at the next intersection and pass one of the Ice Age Trail's dispersed camping areas (DCA). This site is for long distance thru-hikers only. Just beyond the DCA is the picnic area at Badger Prairie County Park—and this route's turnaround point. With restrooms, drinking water, a playground, and shade trees, it's the perfect place to make a pit stop before heading back north. To return to your starting point on McKee Road, follow the route directions in reverse. And take note: the easy descent from the first part of the hike will now be a steady uphill trek.

GO FARTHER

If you're able to use a car shuttle, you can easily link the northern section of the Verona segment to the central section (Trail 27), and to the southern section (Trail 28) beyond that. Instead of turning around at Badger Prairie County Park, hike the half-mile connector route to the next trailhead. Here's how: When you reach the picnic area at Badger Prairie County Park, head to the south end of the parking lot and cross the road. The Ice Age Trail continues on the other side. Turn right (south) onto the paved bike path at 0.2 mile and follow it as it heads south and passes through a tunnel beneath E. Verona Avenue. After exiting the tunnel, turn left (east) and follow the bike path to the Verona Park & Ride, the central section's trailhead.

27 Ice Age Trail: Verona Segment Central

DISTANCE: 3.6 miles
ELEVATION GAIN: 130 feet
HIGH POINT: 1002 feet
DIFFICULTY: Easy
FITNESS: Walkers, hikers, trail runners
FAMILY FRIENDLY: Yes
DOG FRIENDLY: Leashed dogs only
AMENITIES: Parking lot, interpretative info
CONTACT/MAP: Ice Age Trail Alliance; map available online and on-site
GPS: N 42°59'36.0" W 89°30'52.0"
BEFORE YOU GO: Portions of this hike are on multi-use and bike paths; be aware of other trail users.

GETTING THERE

Driving: From Madison, head south on US Highway 18/151 toward Verona. Take exit 81 for Verona Avenue and turn left immediately onto Old County Road PB. Then turn right into the Verona Park & Ride, which is also a trailhead for the Military Hwy Ridge State Trail.

Badger Mill Creek is a small but significant waterway that flows through Verona on its way to the Sugar River. The creek is not only a class 2 trout stream, but also the centerpiece of an environmental and wildlife corridor that connects natural areas within the growing city. The best way to get an up-close look at the creek—and witness its ongoing restoration—is to

Yellow blazes and frequent signs mark the Ice Age Trail

hike the central section of the Ice Age Trail's Verona segment. If you begin and end at the Verona Park & Ride, this out-and-back hike is an easy 3.6 miles on mostly level terrain. Or link this route to the segment's north (Trail 26) and south (Trail 28) sections for a much longer hike along the Ice Age Trail.

GET MOVING

Begin at the southwest corner of the park and ride parking lot and follow the paved bike path south. Just before the bridge, turn right (west) where the paved path intersects with the Military Ridge State Trail. This 40-mile-long recreational trail connects Madison to Dodgeville and is open to both pedestrians and cyclists. For the next quarter mile or so, the route uses the crushed limestone Military Ridge Trail as it parallels Badger Mill Creek. Look for the Ice Age Trail sign and veer left (south) when the hiking trail leaves the Military Ridge Trail and continues along the creek.

At 0.8 mile, cross the pedestrian bridge and hike along the paved bike path for a couple hundred yards until you see the hiking trail enter the woods on the left. Follow this trail over a wooden boardwalk (built by a team of volunteers that included this author) and through the peaceful forest on the southeast side of the creek. Up until a few years ago—as satellite images still attest—forest covered the land from here to the end of this trail segment. Regrettably, many trees along the creek and trail have since been cleared for a sewer construction project, but ecological restoration efforts are underway. At 1.3 miles, the trail rejoins the paved bike path and heads south through the large clearing created by the construction project. Volunteers have re-seeded the area with native plant species. In summer, look for black-eyed Susans, common sunflowers, and coneflowers.

The hiking trail veers left off the bike path again at the 1.4-mile mark. Follow the trail up the hillside as it switchbacks through a forest of stately oaks. It soon emerges from the trees and heads directly to Whalen Road. Although the Ice Age Trail continues beyond Whalen Road, this is the turnaround point for this hike. From here, retrace your steps to your starting point at the Verona Park & Ride for a 3.6-mile roundtrip hike.

GO FARTHER

If you're looking for a challenge, you can hike the central and south sections of the Verona segment together for a

5.8-mile hike from end to end. (The easiest way to do this is to use two vehicles and park a car at each end.) Instead of turning around at Whalen Road, cross the street and follow the hiking trail along the hillside above County Highway M. Use the sidewalk to cross the bridge over Highway 151, then hike along the north side of Highway M. (There can be a lot of traffic, so stay alert.) When you spot the Ice Age Trail parking lot on the south side of the road, carefully cross the street as you watch for cars and bikes. From here, follow the directions for the south section of the Verona segment.

28 Ice Age Trail: Verona Segment South

DISTANCE: 1.6 miles
ELEVATION GAIN: 100 feet
HIGH POINT: 1100 feet
DIFFICULTY: Easy
FITNESS: Walkers, hikers
FAMILY FRIENDLY: Yes
DOG FRIENDLY: Leashed dogs only
AMENITIES: Parking lot, interpretative info
CONTACT/MAP: Ice Age Trail Alliance; map available online and on-site
GPS: N 42°58'19.7" W 89°31'8.2"
BEFORE YOU GO: There are no restrooms or drinking water at this trailhead, so plan ahead.

GETTING THERE

Driving: Take US Highway 18/151 to County Road PB/Old PB (exit 79). Turn left (south) on Old County Highway PB. Turn right (west) onto County Highway M. After 0.7 mile, the trail-head parking lot for the Ice Age Trail's Moraine Kettles Preserve will be on the left.

Not long ago, the trail through Moraine Kettles Preserve was a bramble-choked footpath known for its mosquitoes. But after years of restoration work by dedicated volunteers, this nature preserve now boasts restored prairie and oak woods that surround several ten-thousand-year-old "kettle" ponds. The trail here is part of the Ice Age Trail's Verona segment, but it's also the ideal distance for a short out-and-back hike.

GET MOVING

From the trailhead parking lot, follow the trail southwest, then turn left (south) where this connector trail meets the main Ice Age Trail. From here, the trail curves through one of the preserve's restored prairies as it heads toward the

Oak and hickory woods in Moraine Kettles Preserve

woods. Volunteers sowed thousands of native seeds in this former agricultural field, and in summer and fall it's now bright with forbs and grasses in full bloom. Look for prairie flowers like shooting star and wild bergamot during the growing season.

After the prairie, the trail enters woods that once grew thick with invasive plants, obscuring the deep kettle ponds and crowding out the native species. Today, hickories and century-old oak trees share space with woodland wildflowers like wild geraniums, jack-in-the-pulpit, and Solomon's seal. The kettle ponds tucked within this woodland are potholes created by melting ice at the end of the last ice age. Though small in size, these freshwater habitats provide food and shelter for ducks and other birds—a bald eagle's nest has even been spotted in the area.

At 0.3 mile, the trail passes through a large clearing behind a subdivision before entering the woods again. The last mile or so before the turnaround point is an easy, meandering hike through more oak woods. Just before the 0.8-mile-mark, the trail exits the woods alongside County Highway PB and crosses a driveway; this is this route's turnaround point. Return to the trailhead by following your route in reverse.

GO FARTHER

You can add another 1.5 miles (roundtrip) to this hike by hiking to the official end of the Verona segment. Instead of turning around when the trail reaches Highway PB, head north along the highway as you follow the Ice Age Trail signs. Be extra cautious when crossing Highway PB. There isn't a crosswalk here and there's high-speed traffic. (For that reason, I wouldn't recommend doing this section with children.) The trail continues on the east side of the highway and enters the woods. Follow the yellow blazes and stay right at all junctions. The trail ends at the parking lot for Prairie Moraine County Park.

29 Prairie Moraine County Park

DISTANCE:	3 miles
ELEVATION GAIN:	280 feet
HIGH POINT:	1160 feet
DIFFICULTY:	Moderate
FITNESS:	Hikers
FAMILY FRIENDLY:	Yes
DOG FRIENDLY:	Yes. There is also a large off-leash dog park. A Dane County Parks dog permit is required for both the on-leash and off-leash areas.
AMENITIES:	Parking lot, interpretative info
CONTACT/MAP:	Dane County Parks; map available online and on-site
GPS:	N 42°57'43.6" W 89°30'49.7"

GETTING THERE

Driving: From Madison, head south on US Highway 18/151 toward Verona. Take exit 79 for County Road PB. Turn left (south) on County Road PB. After 1.4 miles, turn left on Wesner Lane, then immediately left into the trailhead parking lot.

Prairie Moraine County Park has one of the largest and most popular dog parks in the Madison area—but this outdoor destination isn't only for dogs and their owners. The park is divided into two distinct halves by a fence. The southern 80 acres is the off-leash dog park with wooded trails, grassy areas, and a designated parking lot. The park's northern half has several (on-leash) hiking trails—including a section of the Ice Age Trail—that meander over and along the park's namesake: a glacial moraine. This 60-foot ridge covered with oak savanna marks the border between Wisconsin's glacier-carved northern landscape and the southern Driftless. Whichever trail you take at this

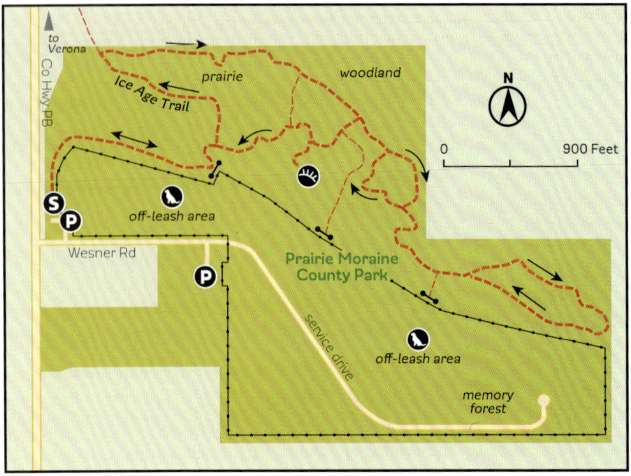

park, don't miss the scenic overlook with views of the Sugar River Valley. And if you'd like to learn more about the landscape as you go, take an interactive watershed trail tour using the GeoTourist app. The tour was created by the Upper Sugar Watershed Association and corresponds to numbered posts along the trail.

GET MOVING

For a 3-mile hike that makes the most of the park's scenery—from moraine to prairie to woodlands—link together a few trails through its northern half. Enter the gate at the trailhead parking lot and head north through the prairie on the Ice Age Trail. From here, you'll have the best view of the moraine as it stretches from east to west. When the prairie is in bloom, you may see native plants like prairie dock and hear grassland birds like song sparrows along this stretch.

Around the 0.25-mile mark, the trail turns north and climbs to the top of the moraine. You'll pass a gate on the right that leads to the off-leash dog park. At 0.4 mile, turn left at the trail intersection. You'll see another prairie on your

Prairie Moraine County Park has both off-leash and on-leash areas for dogs.

right and an oak savanna on your left. The latter habitat type now thrives in the moraine's soil conditions, thanks to twenty years of invasive species removal.

At the next trail intersection, you'll part ways with the Ice Age Trail and head right (east) along the northern edge of the prairie. A business park lies just beyond the border here, so unfortunately you may hear the buildings' loud HVAC systems as you hike. The noise should fade as the trail angles south and enters woodlands again. Keep left when you reach a trail intersection at the 0.9-mile mark, and at the next two trail intersections. For the next quarter mile or so, the trail takes a gently rolling route through the woods near the top of the moraine.

Around 1.2 miles, turn left at the intersection to switchback down a short slope. From here, the trail cuts across a meadow toward another wooded trail loop. At 1.3 miles, turn left to hike the loop in a clockwise direction. The first section is a steady climb through oak woodland and over some rough terrain. After a quarter mile or so, you'll reach the furthest end of the loop. As the trail turns back, it also descends. When the trees are bare, there are some nice views into the southern half of the park.

Once you return to this loop's starting point at 1.8 miles, retrace your route back through the meadow and up the slope. When you reach the trail intersection at the 2-mile mark, turn left rather than retracing your steps, then turn left again at the next trail junction. A short distance down the trail, a bench marks the next junction. Turn left here, then continue straight when another trail veers left. At 2.3 miles, turn left onto the short spur trail to the scenic overlook. This is a serene spot to take a breather or get a better sense of the surrounding landscape.

When you're ready to press on, follow the spur trail back, and turn left at the first trail junction. Stay left again at the next junction to continue heading down the moraine. When you return to the trail intersection at 2.6 miles, you'll be on familiar ground. Turn left to retrace your route back down the moraine and through the prairie to the trailhead.

MAKE IT SHORTER

For a shorter hike where your canine companion can be off leash, try one of the many trails in Prairie Moraine's dog park. Begin at the parking lot at the end of Wessner Lane and enter the off-leash area. If you make a loop using the dog park's outermost trails, it'll be just under 2 miles.

30 Military Ridge State Trail: Verona

DISTANCE:	5 miles
ELEVATION GAIN:	140 feet
HIGH POINT:	980 feet
DIFFICULTY:	Easy
FITNESS:	Walkers, runners, hikers
FAMILY FRIENDLY:	Yes
DOG FRIENDLY:	Leashed dogs only
AMENITIES:	Parking lot, restrooms, drinking water, picnic shelter, athletic fields
CONTACT/MAP:	Wisconsin Department of Natural Resources; map available online
GPS:	N 42°59'32.1" W 89°31'6.0"

GETTING THERE

Driving: From Madison, head south on US Highway 18/151 toward Verona. Take exit 81 for Verona Avenue. Head west on E. Verona Avenue for about 0.4 mile and look for the entrance to Hometown USA Community Park on the left (south) side of the street. This park has several sports fields, so during games or tournaments, parking can fill up quickly. For an alternative starting point, park at the

Walkers and bicyclists share the Military Ridge State Trail.

nearby Verona Park & Ride, where you can also access the Military Ridge State Trail.

The Military Ridge State Trail is a 40-mile recreational trail that runs from the southwest edge of Madison (technically, it starts in Fitchburg) to Dodgeville. As one of the state's many "rails-to-trails" projects—which converted abandoned rail lines into recreational trails—the crushed limestone path is mostly level with a gentle grade. It's popular with cyclists, but its surface and scenery make it an ideal place to hike too. The trail's northernmost section is paved and runs parallel to Highway 151. For a hike that's somewhat close to Madison but much quieter, I recommend hopping on the trail in Verona for a 5-mile out-and-back to Sugar River Wetlands State Natural Area.

GET MOVING

You can access the Military Ridge State Trail from the southern end of the parking lot at Hometown USA Community Park. After taking a short connector path to the trail itself, turn right (west) onto the Military Ridge Trail. For the first 0.4 mile, the tree-lined trail passes behind Community Park.

On the south side of the path, look across the meadow and wetlands to see Badger Mill Creek as it flows south to the Sugar River. About a quarter mile later, the trail nears the heart of downtown Verona and crosses several city streets, including Main Street. The latter can be busy depending on the time of day, so use the pedestrian lights to cross safely. From this point, a couple of coffee shops, a grocery store, and a bookstore are all within a short walk if you're looking for a downtown detour. After crossing Main Street, the trail passes another small public park that has a picnic shelter, restrooms, and drinking water.

Leaving downtown behind, the trail continues under a canopy of trees as it passes through the city. At the 1.7-mile mark, it passes through a short tunnel and reaches the grounds of Verona High School. As you draw closer to Highway 151, you'll likely see signs of ecological restoration in the woods and wetlands. This will become more apparent after passing through a second tunnel (under Highway 18/151) and officially entering Sugar River Wetlands State Natural Area, an expanse of wetlands, prairie, and oak savannas. For many years, volunteers have worked to restore this natural area, parcel by parcel, primarily by uprooting invasive species like buckthorn, honeysuckle, and wild canary grass and helping native plants thrive. Thanks to their work, you can now see plants like prairie blazing star, Culver's root, and asters, along with critically important pollinators like monarch butterflies and various species of bumblebees. Sandhill cranes are also a common sight and sound across this wetland habitat.

The turnaround point for this route is at the 2.4-mile mark, shortly after you enter the wide-open spaces of the state natural area. From here, the Military Ridge Trail continues for another 34 miles to Dodgeville, so you could always walk farther if you'd like—or turn around for the 2.4-mile hike back to the trailhead.

MAKE IT SHORTER

For a hike that's half the distance, turn around where the trail crosses S. Nine Mound Road at the 1.2-mile mark, instead of hiking all the way to Sugar River Wetlands State Natural Area.

31 Donald County Park

DISTANCE:	5.2 miles
ELEVATION GAIN:	400 feet
HIGH POINT:	1110 feet
DIFFICULTY:	Moderate
FITNESS:	Hikers, trail runners
FAMILY FRIENDLY:	Yes
DOG FRIENDLY:	Leashed dogs only; Dane County Parks dog permit required.
AMENITIES:	Parking lot, picnic area and shelter, restrooms, equestrian trails, fishing, interpretative info, historical site
CONTACT/MAP:	Dane County Parks; map available online and on-site
GPS:	N 42°57'31.9" W 89°40'53.8"

GETTING THERE

Driving: From US Highway 12/18, take the exit for Verona Road/US 151 (exit 258) and head south. After 7.9 miles, take exit 75 for County Road G. Drive south on County Road G for 3.5 miles, then turn right onto Messerschmidt Road. After 1.8 miles, turn right onto State Highway 92. Pass the entrance for Pop's Knoll on the left and continue to Sutter Drive. Turn left onto Sutter and drive the short distance to the Deer Creek parking lot and trailhead.

In the 1990s, two longtime farming families—the Donald/Woodburn and Hitchcock families—sold their land to create a public county park. Today their combined 775 acres of idyllic Wisconsin countryside not only encompass forests, rock

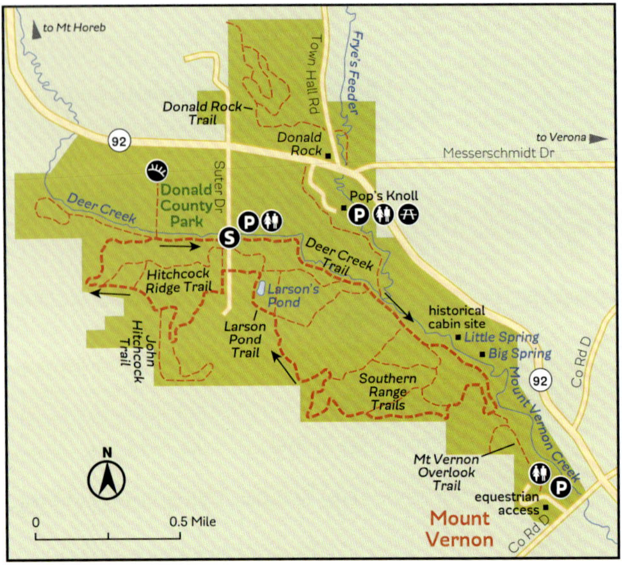

outcroppings, prairies, and trout streams, but also holds a deeper history. An archaeological dig in the early 2000s unearthed incredible evidence of the land's much earlier inhabitants, including a nine-thousand-year-old spear point made by Paleo-Indians. One of my favorite hikes at this park is a meandering route that follows Deer Creek, pauses at the historical springs and archaeological site, and winds through prairies and forests. The recommended trailhead for this route doesn't have restrooms, so stop at Pop's Knoll picnic area beforehand, where there are vault toilets. Alternatively, you can also access several hiking trails from Pop's Knoll, including this route.

GET MOVING

This hike begins at the Deer Creek trailhead (Deer Creek Fishing Access), where the trail departs from the east end of the parking lot, paralleling Deer Creek for nearly a mile. With

An observation deck at Donald County Park's Big Spring

the lively trout stream gurgling alongside and shade trees overhead, it's a relaxing place to stroll. Stay straight when two consecutive trails branch off to the right. At 0.7 mile, the North Access Trail enters from the left. For a closer look at Deer Creek, take a brief detour down the hill to the wooden bridge; otherwise, continue hiking east. There are several apple trees growing along the trail here, many planted long ago by park cofounder Delma Woodburn. Foraging is allowed, and along with wild apples, there are black and red raspberries, gooseberries, and blackberries throughout the summer.

Stay straight at 0.9 mile when a trail branches right. In another 0.1 mile, veer left at the fork into a grassy area with several more apple trees. This is Little Spring, one of the park's historical sites, where you can see the restored foundation of an 1850s cabin and the spring itself. At the east end of the site, the trail continues into the woods. Big Spring is about a quarter mile beyond Little Spring. This crystal-clear pool surrounded by pines is best viewed from the wooden platform on its east side, where there's interpretative info about the spring's history.

After Big Spring, continue through the woods and you'll reach a trail intersection at 1.5 miles. Turn right (west), following the trail as it skirts the edge of the woods—prime raspberry habitat. Black raspberries are abundant here, but there are red raspberries too. Turn left (south) at 1.9 miles; after a few hundred feet, the trail turns west. For the next mile or so, travel through a peaceful forest of broadleaf trees like shagbark hickory and black cherry. Keep left at both trail junctions in this section.

At 3.1 miles, you'll reach a fragrant grove of red and Scotch pines. Just beyond, the forest opens up and you'll hike through two consecutive trail intersections. Keep left at both. Then at 3.3 miles, turn right (north). After passing more woods, you'll see Larson's Pond ahead on the right. A bench here offers the opportunity to rest and take in the view. Follow the trail along the west side of the pond, then turn left (west) at the next trail intersection and climb through a prairie packed with wildflowers during the summer and fall. Look for bright orange butterfly weed and the yellow flowers of the compass plant, the tallest in the prairie.

On the far side of this prairie, the trail crosses Sutter Drive. Once you reach the other side of the road, go left (south) at the intersection. After the trail turns right (west) at 3.6 miles, it climbs through sumac and blackberry bushes, then traverses another small forest. At 3.9 miles, turn right (north) and follow the trail as it winds through several agricultural fields. Keep right at 4.1 miles, then stay left at the next two intersections. At 4.5 miles, the trail turns into the woods. About a quarter mile later, it intersects with the Sweet Farm Trail, a mowed trail. Turn right (east) to follow this trail back to your starting point at the Deer Creek Fishing Access parking lot.

MAKE IT SHORTER

There are several ways to shorten this hike if you're not up for the entire 5.2 miles. The first is to do an out-and-back hike from the Deer Creek trailhead to Big Spring. The roundtrip distance for this is 2.4 miles. For a hike that's just over 3.5 miles, follow this route to where it crosses Sutter Road at the 3.5-mile mark. Instead of crossing the road here, turn right onto the road and walk the short distance back to the parking lot.

Next page: Dorn Creek flows into Six Mile Creek in Governor Nelson State Park (Trail 32)

NORTHWEST

With lakes at its center, and communities that often blend seamlessly into one another, it can be a challenge to divide the Madison area into neatly defined regions. That's one reason you'll see some cities, like Waunakee, in more than one section of this book. For our purposes, the Madison area's northwest region begins at the northwest shore of Lake Mendota and includes cities and towns at the edge of the Driftless Area to the west. The Driftless, also known as "bluff country," is a sweep of land that was never covered by ice in the last ice age. As a result, the geography is distinct from the glacier-shorn areas around it and is marked by ridges, ravines, bluffs, forests, and more than 13,000 miles of cold-water trout streams. Most of the Driftless is in Wisconsin, but it also extends into parts of Minnesota and Iowa. It's not only an angler's paradise, it's a hiker's too, with miles of trails and more than twenty sections of the Ice Age National Scenic Trail. The northwest region of Madison is also where you'll find the only state park on Lake Mendota—Governor Nelson State Park—along with conservancies, county parks, and an eco-minded monastery with grounds open to the public.

32 Governor Nelson State Park: Morningside Trail

DISTANCE: 2.4 miles
ELEVATION GAIN: 160 feet
HIGH POINT: 950 feet
DIFFICULTY: Easy to moderate
FITNESS: Hikers, walkers, trail runners
FAMILY FRIENDLY: Yes
DOG FRIENDLY: Leashed dogs allowed on hiking trails; no dogs allowed at the swimming beach or picnic area, but there is a separate pet swim area.
AMENITIES: Parking lot, restrooms, picnic area, shelters, boat launch, swimming, fishing, interpretive info, pet swim area, accessible fishing pier
CONTACT/MAP: Governor Nelson State Park; map available online
GPS: N 43°7'59.0" W 89°26'5.4"
BEFORE YOU GO: A state park vehicle admission sticker (daily or annual) is required year-round. In winter, the hiking trails are groomed for cross-country skiing and snowshoeing.

GETTING THERE

Driving: From US Highway 12 in Middleton, take the Airport Road/County Highway M exit (exit 250) and head east. Continue on Highway M for 5.6 miles; the state park entrance will be on your left. Purchase a vehicle admission sticker at the park office, then continue driving to the first parking lot on your left (after the park office parking lot). This is one of the access points for the Morningside Trail.

Across the lake from Madison's busy downtown and university, Governor Nelson State Park is a place to experience the quieter side of Lake Mendota. Most people come to this 422-acre park with boats and fishing gear in tow—its forested shoreline includes a boat launch, fishing pier, swimming beach, and pet swim area. But the park's less-explored interior is worth a visit too, with more than 8 miles of hiking and biking trails that traverse woods, wetlands, and prairie. (In the midst of this landscape, hikers can also see several earthen mounds—including a panther effigy mound—created by the ancestral Ho-Chunk people.) While the hum of traffic on nearby Highway M is never far away, the cool woods and lake breezes at this wildlife haven make it an ideal destination for a warm-weather ramble.

GET MOVING

For a prairie hike with an optional lakefront detour, try the 2.4-mile Morningside Trail. Begin at the trailhead in the state park's northern parking lot and follow the paved path toward Lake Mendota. Ahead of you is the state park's main picnic area and swimming beach, a great post-hike place to cool off. When you see the sign for the Morningside Trail, turn left to follow

Osprey nesting platform and interpretive panel on the Morningside Trail

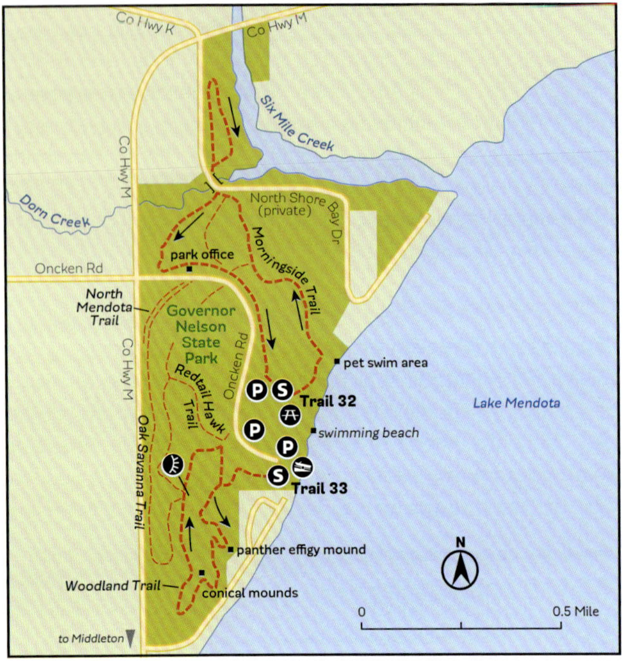

the trail into the woods. At 0.2 mile, you'll pass the designated pet swim area on your right.

Angling away from the lake, the Morningside Trail heads northwest through open prairie and wetlands. This is an ideal place to see and hear birds, including sandhill cranes. At 0.6 mile, a connector trail veers left (west), but continue hiking straight (northwest). As you pass several large oaks on the west side of the trail at 0.8 mile, look for an elevated platform in the meadow beyond. In spring or early summer, you might see a pair of nesting ospreys, also known as fish hawks, and their chicks.

After passing another connector trail on the left, the main hiking trail intersects a paved bike path and a private road (North Shore Bay Drive) in a cul-de-sac at 0.8 mile. (The paved path is the 4-mile North Mendota Trail that connects Waunakee to the state park.) Watch for cars and bikes as you walk through the cul-de-sac and cross the bridge over Dorn Creek. To the right (east), Dorn Creek flows into Six Mile Creek and the wetlands along Lake Mendota. After crossing the bridge, pick up the hiking trail again on the right side of the road and stay left to hike a 0.6-mile loop through a prairie. When you complete this loop, you'll be back at North Shore Bay Drive. Turn left (south) to cross Dorn Creek again and return to the cul-de-sac. Back at the trail intersection, head right (west) on the paved bike path for 0.1 mile until you reach the mowed trail of the Morningside Trail. On this return loop, the trail passes through prairie, then parallels the park's main road back to the parking lot where you started. Once you've returned to your starting point, you can take the short paved path to the lakefront's picnic area and swimming beach for a post-hike swim.

33 Governor Nelson State Park: Woodland Trail

DISTANCE: 1.6 miles
ELEVATION GAIN: 120 feet
HIGH POINT: 950 feet
DIFFICULTY: Easy to moderate
FITNESS: Hikers, walkers, trail runners
FAMILY FRIENDLY: Yes
DOG FRIENDLY: Leashed dogs allowed on hiking trails; no dogs allowed at the swimming beach or picnic area, but there is a separate pet swim area.
AMENITIES: Parking lot, restrooms, picnic area, shelters, boat launch, swimming, fishing, interpretive info, pet swim area, accessible fishing pier
CONTACT/MAP: Governor Nelson State Park; map available online
GPS: N 43°7'47.6" W 89°26'5.2"
BEFORE YOU GO: A state park vehicle admission sticker (daily or annual) is required year-round.

GETTING THERE

Driving: From US Highway 12 in Middleton, take the Airport Road/County Highway M exit (exit 250) and head east. Continue on Highway M for 5.6 miles; the state park entrance will be on your left. Purchase a vehicle admission sticker at the park office, then continue to the last parking lot on your left near the boat launch.

Hidden away in the southern end of Governor Nelson State Park, it can be easy to miss the quiet Woodland Trail. But this 1.6-mile loop is packed with wildflowers in the spring, cool and green during the summer, and crackling with colorful leaves in the fall. (And in the winter, it's groomed for cross-country skiing and snowshoeing.) In short, there's never a bad time to add this loop to your hiking itinerary. The forest is also home to several earthen mounds, including a panther effigy, created by the ancestral Ho-Chunk people. You can learn more about them, and the area's history, by picking up a printed guide at the trailhead kiosk.

GET MOVING

Start at the state park's southernmost parking lot. Walk the paved road leading from the eastern end of the lot until it meets the park's main road. The Woodland Trail begins on the opposite side of this road and is a hilly 1.6-mile loop designed as a self-guided nature walk with numbered markers. After passing the Woodland Trail sign, take a left at the T intersection to follow the loop in a clockwise direction. Before the trees leaf out in spring, this south-facing section of the trail is bursting with woodland wildflowers like trout lilies, Dutchman's breeches, mayapples, and violets.

At 0.4 mile, a sign directs you to the first of several earthen mounds made by the ancestral Ho-Chunk people. The first is an effigy mound created in the shape of a panther. A quarter mile down the trail, you'll see a sign for a group of conical

Early spring on the Woodland Trail

mounds. At the bottom of the loop, the trail turns north and gains elevation until you reach an overlook with benches. (Unfortunately, you can't see much more than treetops from this high vantage point, but it's still a nice place to take in the scenery.) The Oak Savanna Trail both enters and exits at the overlook, so as you continue on the route, be sure to bear right (northeast) to stay on the Woodland Trail. At 1.3 miles, the trail meets the Redtail Hawk Trail, but bear right to follow the Woodland Trail back to the trailhead.

GO FARTHER

To be a Governor Nelson State Park completist, hike the Morningside Trail, Woodland Trail, Oak Savanna Trail (1.8 miles), and Redtail Hawk Trail (1 mile) in one go. Each of the park's four hiking trails intersect with one or two of the other trails, making it easy to link them together for an extra-long day hike that's just under 7 miles.

SAVING OUR WILD PLACES

When you hike in the Madison area, you'll see native wildflowers blooming in places that were once depleted farm fields, and you'll follow trails through woods that were once choked by invasives. As you read the route descriptions in this guide, you'll see repeated references to "restored" habitats such as prairies and savannas. The wild places highlighted in this guide exist because people had either the foresight to protect them from development, or the vision and tenacity to restore them. We owe a debt of gratitude to the people—many of them volunteers—who've dedicated their time and energy to not only preserving and restoring our natural world, but to making it accessible to us by creating trails and maintaining them.

As you explore our community, one trail at a time, you'll also notice that the ecological work isn't finished. You'll see lakes scummy with algae blooms, roadsides where people leave their trash, trail facilities in need of repair, and natural areas threatened by development. In cities, there's always ongoing tension between expanding the human-built world (of homes, businesses, and infrastructure) and protecting nature. If you want to be a part of protecting and restoring nature, here are local organizations to check out (see Resources for contact information):

- **Dane County Parks Friends Groups:** These are groups of volunteers who give their time and energy to care for a specific Dane County park.
- **State Park Friends Groups:** These are groups of volunteers who give their time and energy to care for a specific state park.
- **Ice Age Trail Alliance:** This nonprofit oversees the development and maintenance of the Ice Age Trail and offers many volunteer opportunities through the year.
- **Wisconsin Master Naturalist Program:** This program promotes environmental stewardship and citizen science by equipping people to become trained conservation volunteers.
- **Southern Wisconsin Bird Alliance:** This is the south-central Wisconsin chapter of the National Audubon Society; it offers ways to get involved through membership or volunteer opportunities.

34 Holy Wisdom Monastery

DISTANCE: 2.3 miles
ELEVATION GAIN: 170 feet
HIGH POINT: 980 feet
DIFFICULTY: Easy
FITNESS: Walkers, hikers, trail runners
FAMILY FRIENDLY: Yes
DOG FRIENDLY: Dogs not allowed
AMENITIES: Parking lot, restrooms (in monastery), benches, interpretative info
CONTACT/MAP: Holy Wisdom Monastery and Dane County Parks; maps available online and on-site
GPS: N 43°7'19.1" W 89°27'9.5"

GETTING THERE

Driving: From University Avenue in Madison, turn right (north) onto Allen Boulevard. After a mile, turn right (east) onto County Highway M. Drive 2 miles, and the entrance to Holy Wisdom Monastery will be your left. Keep right at the first fork and follow the road to the upper parking lot. The trailhead is on the north side of the parking lot.

For more than sixty years, Holy Wisdom Monastery has been a place of rest and spiritual renewal on a sunny hillside overlooking Lake Mendota. Although it was founded by Benedictine sisters as a girls' high school in the 1950s, the sisters later re-opened the site as an ecumenical retreat and conference center with an emphasis on community and care for the Earth. Since the 1990s, the sisters, staff, and volunteers have worked to restore the 130-acre property to a vibrant native landscape by planting prairies, clearing invasives from oak savannas and woodlands, and unearthing the aptly named Lost Lake, a glacial lake that had been filled with sediment. Four miles of hiking trails traverse the monastery's grounds and connect to trails in the adjacent North Mendota Wildlife Area. These well-marked trails are free and open to the public and can be accessed from the north side of the parking lot behind the main monastery building.

GET MOVING

See the highlights of Holy Wisdom's restoration work—and a scenic Lake Mendota view—on this double-loop hike through the monastery grounds and North Mendota Wildlife Area. Starting at the trailhead kiosk, head northeast up the hill to the overlook. Here you'll find a bench and a panoramic view of Lake Mendota—on a clear day, you can see Wisconsin's capitol building to the east and UW–Madison's campus. From here, head downhill away from the lake and cross the gravel service road. You'll pick up the trail on the other side as it enters a savanna, then turns into the woods. For roughly the next quarter mile, keep left at the next two intersections as the trail meanders through forest (first pines, then maples and other hardwoods).

At 0.3 mile, turn right and follow the trail into the prairie, crossing into the North Mendota Wildlife Area. Due to recent development, the prairie is now hemmed in by houses on two sides—some maps still show farmland here—but it's still a pretty place to walk. Turn left (west) at the next trail intersection and stay on the mowed trail as it follows the prairie's perimeter, turning eastward at 0.5 mile. Continue hiking east until a trail intersection at 0.8 mile. Turn right (south) at this junction. In summer, this section of the hike is full of sunflowers and black-eyed Susans.

Stay straight when you reach a four-way trail intersection at 0.9 mile, then continue straight again at a three-way

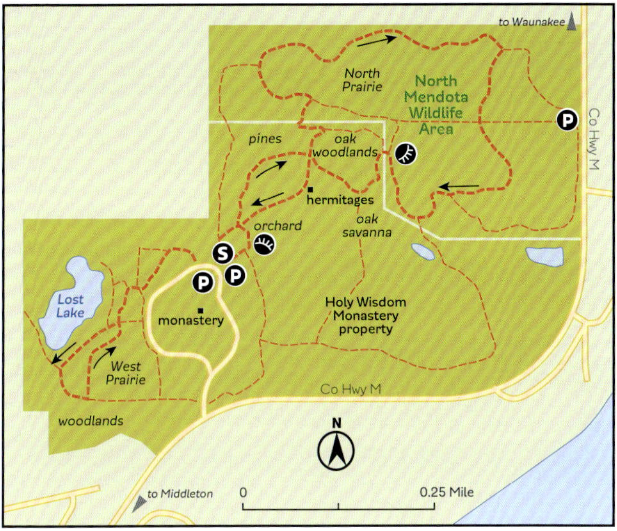

intersection, following the trail as it turns north. Turn left (west) at 1.2 miles where a trail enters the woods. You'll pass another bench and return to the monastery's property as you do. Shortly after this point, stay right again to stay on the route as you hike through forest, then turn left when you reach another intersection at 1.4 miles. As you exit the woods, you'll emerge onto the gravel service road and pass the monastery's hermitages (guest houses). Follow the service road back to the spot where you crossed it the first time and retrace your steps south to the Lake Mendota overlook, then down the hill to the trailhead.

Start this route's second loop by heading west from the trailhead kiosk and following the paved driveway down to another parking lot. Find the trail at the eastern end of this parking lot and follow it past the monastery's garden and orchard. At 1.6 miles, the trail enters the woods on the south side of a gravel service road and passes beneath some beautiful old pine trees. When the trail exits these

The hike at Holy Wisdom Monastery begins with a beautiful view of Lake Mendota.

woods and continues through prairie, you'll get a first look at Lost Lake, which was nearly filled in by sediment from surrounding development before the Benedictine community dredged and restored it in the 1990s. This lake plays an important part in the local watershed, filtering water that drains from more than 200 acres of land.

As you exit the woods at 1.7 miles, head southwest to follow a mowed trail that parallels the lake. There are several benches along this section. Stay right at the next trail junction, then keep left as the trail passes through woods and makes a wide 180-degree turn. Turn left (north) at 1.9 miles to hike between the woods and prairie. Above the wildflowers to your right, you'll see the monastery's retreat center up the hill. At 2 miles, keep straight and retrace your route back through the woods, past the monastery garden, and along the driveway back to the trailhead parking lot.

MAKE IT SHORTER

For an easier hike with plenty of benches, walk only the second loop of this route, beginning and ending at the main trailhead. It's about 0.75 mile roundtrip and a particularly good route for young children who are new to hiking.

35 Pope Farm Conservancy

DISTANCE:	1.7 miles
ELEVATION GAIN:	180 feet
HIGH POINT:	1180 feet
DIFFICULTY:	Easy to moderate
FITNESS:	Walkers, hikers, trail runners
FAMILY FRIENDLY:	Yes
DOG FRIENDLY:	Dogs not allowed
AMENITIES:	Parking lot, restrooms (seasonal), drinking water (seasonal), interpretative info
CONTACT/MAP:	Friends of Pope Farm Conservancy; map available online and on-site
GPS:	N 43°4'39.3" W 89°33'57.7"

GETTING THERE

Driving: From US Highway 12 in Middleton, take the exit for Old Sauk Road (exit 253) and head west. After 2.3 miles, turn right into Pope Farm Conservancy. There are two parking lots, lower and upper, and both have access to the conservancy's hiking trails. For the route described in this guide, follow the driveway up and around the hill, and park in the upper parking lot. This route can also be accessed from the lower parking lot via a connector trail. From the lower parking lot, head north on the gravel trail that runs parallel to the stone fence until you reach the upper parking lot. Note: The upper parking lot closes thirty minutes before sunset and is gated.

In the not-too-distant past, family farms filled the countryside around Madison. But now, as that same countryside is filled with neighborhoods and commercial development, those farms—and the natural features they often stewarded—continue to disappear. Pope Farm in the Town of Middleton is an exception. In the early 2000s, the township and the last farmers of the land, Art and Betty Pope, worked together to set aside Pope Farm as a conservancy. Today these 105 acres of prairies, farmland, and woods are a public greenspace and outdoor classroom. And while many people come to the conservancy for its 7 miles of winding trails, the best part may be its view. The park's highest point, just beyond the upper parking lot, reveals a panorama of downtown Madison to the east and the rolling hills of the Driftless to the north and west. Take the time to watch a sunrise or sunset here—hike or no hike.

GET MOVING

From the upper parking lot, head north and pass through the gap in the massive stone fence that cuts through the property. The fence isn't decorative, although it *does* add to the scenery. It was first built by farmers nearly two hundred years ago. The stones came from the surrounding fields, dug from the dirt and hoisted into place over three decades. After you pass through the fence—and admire its longevity—turn right to follow the trail north. Then stay straight at the next intersection when another trail heads west.

At 0.2 mile, you'll reach another trail intersection at the top of a shortgrass prairie. Beyond it, you'll see the hills and valleys of the Black Earth Creek watershed, one of three watersheds that begin on this land. Head north down the hill—you'll see a conservancy parking lot ahead of you on Blackhawk Road—then turn left (west) at the next trail junction. Several short connector trails cut through the prairie; just keep heading straight (west) at all junctions until the trail reaches the woods and turns south around 0.4 mile. Follow the trail south—and up!—along the ravine; this is the steepest section of the hike. At the top, turn right (west).

Continue heading west on the trail for 0.3 mile as it passes forested private property on one side and active agricultural fields on the other. Depending on the year, you may see corn, soybeans, or other crops growing here. Stay straight (west) at

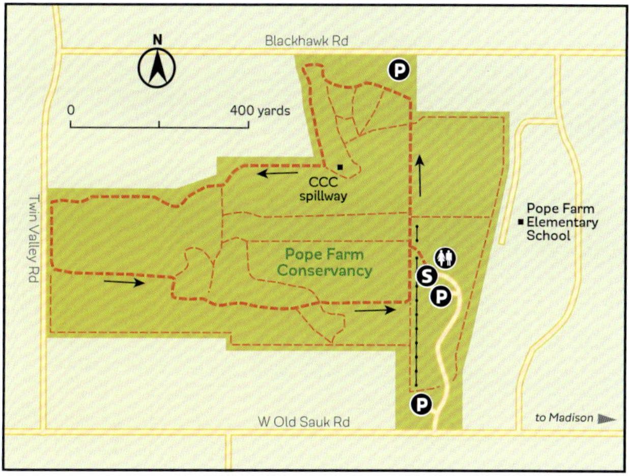

The stone fence at Pope Farm is more than 200 years old.

all trail junctions until you reach the white rail fence that runs along the western edge of the park. When you reach the fence at the 1-mile mark, turn left to follow the trail south along the park's border. At the next intersection, turn left onto the mowed trail that cuts between two farm fields. When you see a hill with maple trees up ahead, follow the trail around the hill to the right.

Head straight at the next intersection and you'll see a long, low ridge with oak trees scattered along it. This oak savanna is an example of a habitat type that was once common in southern Wisconsin. At 1.4 miles, veer left and up into the oak savanna, passing into another farm field on the other side. From here, the trail heads straight east to the stone fence. Once you reach it, head north to the gap. Pass through and go back to the upper parking lot.

MAKE IT SHORTER

A lesser-used trailhead is located on Blackhawk Road on the north side of the conservancy. The Deep Ravine Loop that begins here is just 0.6 mile but also links up with other trails.

36 Pheasant Branch Conservancy

DISTANCE: 4.2 miles
ELEVATION GAIN: 240 feet
HIGH POINT: 1050 feet
DIFFICULTY: Easy to moderate
FITNESS: Walkers, hikers, trail runners
FAMILY FRIENDLY: Yes, but there are some steps and steep segments on Frederick's Hill Trail.
DOG FRIENDLY: Leashed dogs only
AMENITIES: Parking lot, restrooms, interpretive info, benches
CONTACT/MAP: Dane County Parks; map available online
GPS: N 43°7'10.5" W 89°28'39.7"

GETTING THERE

Driving: The trailhead for this hike is at Orchid Heights Park. From Madison, head north on US Highway 12 to the County Highway M/Century Avenue exit (exit 250). Head east on Highway M/Century Avenue for 2 miles. Turn left on Valley Ridge Road and in just over half a mile, turn left on Sedge-meadow Road. Then take a final left on Park Trail, which leads into the public parking lot at Orchid Heights Park.

Beyond the suburban buzz of Middleton is a world of wildflower meadows, tranquil woods, and lively wetlands. At more than 500 acres, Pheasant Branch Conservancy is an oasis for animals, plants, and people. Sandhill cranes, herons, white-tailed deer, foxes, and bald eagles are a few of the many animals you might see. Whether your sojourn is long or short, a hike through the conservancy offers a chance to see centuries-old bur oak trees, an active prairie restoration, and the springs that supply fresh water to nearby Lake Mendota. The conservancy can be accessed via several trailheads, but I recommend the trailhead at Orchid Heights Park because it has public restrooms and the largest parking lot. The other main trailhead is just off Pheasant Branch Drive on the conservancy's west side.

GET MOVING

For a 4.2-mile hike that includes the popular trek up Frederick's Hill and a loop through the conservancy, begin at the Orchid Heights Park. From the parking lot, head north on the park's entrance road and look for the gravel trail heading northwest into the prairie. This is where this hike begins. For the first half mile, the trail is straight and level as it passes through sedge meadow and prairie, ideal for strollers and wheelchairs. This portion of the hike is on a multi-use trail, so be aware of approaching users from either direction, especially bikes. About 0.4 mile from the trailhead, you can glimpse Frederick Springs, the headwaters of Pheasant Branch Creek, through the trees on your left. For a closer look, and a brief detour, take the trail on the left that heads down the hill to the observation deck above the springs. Look closely into the clear, shallow pond to see the telltale signs of the springs: trails of bubbles swirling up from the sandy bottom. If you've taken this detour, retrace your steps to return to the main route.

Just beyond the springs overlook, you'll reach a trail junction. Follow the Frederick's Hill Trail as it takes a sharp right (north) toward the hill itself. The next half mile of the trail is narrower and steeper as it circles the hill and makes

Frederick's Hill at Pheasant Branch Conservancy

a couple of switchbacks before reaching the top. At 1050 feet, Frederick's Hill is the park's highest point, and from this vantage point among the oaks, hikers can see Lake Mendota in the distance, and on a clear day, the white dome of the Wisconsin State Capitol. Catch the views at two scenic overlooks before heading down the way you came.

Back at the trail junction at the 1.4-mile mark, turn right to hop on the conservancy's main loop. This multi-use trail (that's alternately paved and crushed stone) roughly follows the perimeter of the conservancy. Keep left at all trail junctions to follow the trail for 2.7 miles back to your starting point. Along the way you'll pass through meadows, woods, and wetlands.

GO FARTHER

The Pheasant Branch Creek Corridor Trail is a multi-use, accessible path that branches off the southern end of the conservancy's main loop and follows Pheasant Branch Creek as it meanders through Middleton. Add this 3-mile out-and-back trek to the above route for a long-distance hike, or try it as a standalone hike. From its junction with the conservancy's main loop (2.8 miles into the 4.2-mile hike described in the previous section), follow the Pheasant Branch Creek Corridor Trail approximately 0.3 mile south to Highway M. Cross the highway at the signal, then turn right and follow the sidewalk a short distance to the trail, which will be on your left. Follow the trail for another 1.2 miles as it parallels Pheasant Branch Creek. There are several shallow creek crossings with bridges (or try the stepping stones if you're up for it). When the trail reaches Parmenter Street at the 4.3-mile mark, turn around and retrace your steps back to the conservancy. Although the trail continues and eventually links with other Middleton multi-use trails, this is the most scenic section and a good turnaround spot.

37 Festge County Park

DISTANCE:	3.5 miles
ELEVATION GAIN:	340 feet
HIGH POINT:	1040 feet
DIFFICULTY:	Moderate, with some easy sections
FITNESS:	Hikers, walkers, trail runners
FAMILY FRIENDLY:	Yes, but there are some steep and narrow sections.
DOG FRIENDLY:	Leashed dogs only; Dane County Parks dog permit required.
AMENITIES:	Parking lot, picnic areas, shelters, restrooms, playground, scenic overlooks, interpretive signs
CONTACT/MAP:	Dane County Parks; map available online
GPS:	N 43°7'18.5" W 89°41'3.5"
BEFORE YOU GO:	The park is open for deer bow-hunting and turkey hunting seasons (September to January). If you hike during this time, wear blaze orange and stay alert. If hiking with your dog, keep it leashed and dress it in blaze orange too.

GETTING THERE

Driving: From US Highway 12 in Middleton, take exit 251A for US Highway 14/University Avenue and head west on Highway 14. Drive 9.5 miles (through Cross Plains), then turn right on Scherbel Road. After 0.3 mile, the park entrance and first parking area will be on the right.

The trails at Festge County Park will one day link to the nearby Table Bluff segment of the Ice Age Trail. In the meantime, with around 4 miles of hiking trails, there's still much to explore within this bluff-top park—from verdant oak and hickory woodlands to prairies busy with pollinators. Most of the park's 155 acres can be explored on foot, thanks to several interconnected trails that wind through the landscape. That said, an abundance of trail junctions can make navigation tricky, so keep a map handy and follow trail signage. The park also has several picnic areas and scenic overlooks that offer

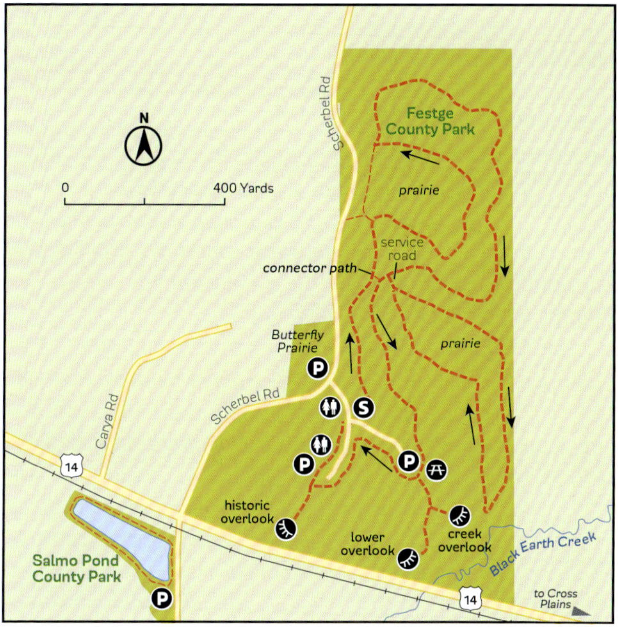

a bird's-eye view of the meandering Black Earth Creek. (Two overlooks can be reached by a paved road.) And speaking of birds, bring your binoculars. Festge is a haven for several woodpecker species and other colorful birds like indigo buntings, cardinals, orioles, and eastern bluebirds.

GET MOVING

For a grand tour of the park's woodland and prairie habitats, hike a 3.5-mile circuit that combines three loops and begins near the main parking lot on Scherbel Road. From the park entrance, follow the paved road to the left. Just beyond a restroom building, a hiking trail enters the woods on the left side of the road—look for the "Nature Trail" sign.

The first section of this hike passes under mature oaks and hickories. In the spring and summer, native wildflowers like trilliums, columbines, and violets bloom along the trail, and if you time it right, you may even see morels and chicken of the woods mushrooms. (Note: Foraging for wild edibles like these is allowed in Dane County Parks as long as it's for personal use only and you follow park guidelines.) At 0.2 mile, keep heading left (north) where a connector trail branches right. After a few hundred feet, the woods open to a prairie and you'll reach a T intersection. Turn right (east) and follow the gently sloping mowed trail along the prairie's edge.

The trail circles the prairie for about a half mile before reaching another intersection. Turn right (north) to head toward the woods. (If you'd prefer a shorter hike or are hiking with young children, turn left at this intersection instead; a short connector trail will take you to the place where you first exited the woods on the opposite side of the prairie. Then retrace your route through the woods back to the trailhead. Roundtrip distance for this shorter hike is just under 1.5 miles.)

The next mile through the woods includes the steepest and most narrow sections of the hike—it's also where you're more likely to see wildlife like white-tailed deer. At 1.5 miles, the trail intersects a gravel service road. Turn left (south) and follow the gravel road down to the prairie below. From this vantage point, you can see the next mile of the route as it makes a wide circle around the prairie, but this unique habitat is worth a closer look. Like other prairies in the park, this is a prairie remnant, a native grassland habitat that has never been farmed or otherwise disturbed by humans—a rarity in most of the US. From midsummer to fall, it's full of wildflowers and native grasses.

After completing the prairie loop and returning to the intersection of the trail and service road, turn left (south), heading up and into the woods. For the next quarter mile, the trail runs parallel along the bluff, the tall trees and open understory allowing beautiful views into the prairie

The prairie at Festge County Park is a rare "prairie remnant."

below. Take a short detour to the Creek View overlook if you'd like, then continue to where the trail ends around 2.8 miles at the Lower Overlook. This scenic overlook affords a 180-degree view of Driftless Area hills and farmland. To continue the hike, retrace your route to the overlook parking lot, then follow the trail that veers left (northwest). This will take you to the neighboring overlook to the west. From this third overlook, retrace your route until you reach the park's paved road, then follow it a short distance back to the trailhead and your starting point.

GO FARTHER

For a closer look at Black Earth Creek, a world-class trout stream, stop by Salmo Pond just across Highway 14 from Festge County Park. Fishing is the focus at this tiny county park with a 3-acre lake, creek access, three ADA-accessible fishing piers, and two ADA-accessible shore fishing stations. There's also a picnic area and a 0.4-mile path around the lake if you want to hike just a bit more.

38 Ice Age Trail: Cross Plains Segment

DISTANCE: 3.1 miles
ELEVATION GAIN: 430 feet
HIGH POINT: 1110 feet
DIFFICULTY: Moderate
FITNESS: Hikers
FAMILY FRIENDLY: Yes, but more suitable for older children.
DOG FRIENDLY: Leashed dogs only
AMENITIES: None on-site; restrooms and other amenities available in town.
CONTACT/MAP: Ice Age Trail Alliance; map available online
GPS: N 43°7'5.8" W 89°39'7.7"

GETTING THERE

Driving: From Middleton, head west on US Highway 14 toward Cross Plains. After 6.5 miles, turn right onto Hickory Street. Proceed for 0.2 miles and turn left onto Hickory Hill Street. The entrance for Hickory Hill Conservancy, and the start of this route, is at the north end of Hickory Hill Street.

Stretching from western Dane County to the Mississippi River, Wisconsin's Driftless Area is known for its natural beauty: forested bluffs, wild prairies, and churning creeks make this region a hiker's paradise. To get a taste of what the Driftless has to offer, hike the Cross Plains segment of the Ice Age Trail; it's a short drive from Madison. The segment's endpoints are in a residential neighborhood, and the trail itself twists and turns above town—but don't let its closeness to town fool you. A few steps up the trail and you'll be in a wilder world full of songbirds and solitude.

GET MOVING

For an energizing 3.1-mile circuit, hike the Cross Plains segment from end-to-end, then take a short walk through a neighborhood to return to your starting point. From the trailhead at the end of Hickory Hill Street, head north up the service road. You'll pass signs for both Hickory Hill Conservancy Park and the Ice Age Trail. For about the first quarter mile, the trail makes a steady climb through the woods. At 0.3 mile, turn left at the junction. This short out-and-back spur trail passes through forest before ending at a scenic overlook above Cross Plains. Once you've seen the view, retrace your steps to the junction and veer left to continue on the main trail.

Soon a hidden hilltop prairie comes into view as you enter the S. B. Andersen Memorial Preserve. This prairie is a refuge for grassland-loving plants and wildlife like beeblossom and eastern bluebirds. Keep left when a connector trail veers right

The Ice Age Trail's Cross Plains segment passes through oak and hickory forest.

at 0.8 mile, and head deeper into the tall grasses and wildflowers. With woodlands along its borders and long views into the hills beyond, this protected meadow has a secluded feel despite its proximity to town. As you enter the woods again at 1.1 miles, you'll see a trail veering to the left. This is the entrance to Andersen Preserve's Dispersed Camping Area (DCA), a place that's been set aside for long-distance multi-day Ice Age Trail hikers who need a place to camp for the night. Veer right to continue the route as it heads down into the forest. For the next half mile or so, the trail passes through several scenic ridges and gullies. Known as Three Gorges, this section remains as lush as a rainforest even on dry summer days. In July and August, the hillsides and hollows here are green with cascading ferns and carpets of mosses.

At 1.5 miles, the trail switchbacks and begins to climb through a basswood forest. A short time later, the trail once again crosses the Andersen Preserve's prairie. Continue left toward the trees ahead when a connector trail turns right at the 1.8-mile mark. From there it's a downhill ramble through a savanna that gradually becomes a forest of oaks and hickories. A private trail branches to the right at 2.1 miles, but continue straight to stay on route (and public land). You'll reach the hike's second overlook at 2.5 miles, where there's a bench to enjoy the view. From here, the trail descends through switchbacks and steep steps to reach the neighborhood below. Right before the trail ends, it emerges from the woods and passes between private property before leading to Lewis Street. Watch for cars as you turn right onto Lewis Street, then take a left on Cross Street. After about a quarter mile, turn right onto Hickory Hill Street to return to your starting point.

If hiking the Cross Plains segment piques your curiosity about the Ice Age Trail, or you're interested in thru hiking, you're in the right place. The Ice Age Trail Alliance's headquarters are a short stroll (or drive) away at 2110 Main Street in Cross Plains.

GO FARTHER

The Cross Plains segment doesn't end at Lewis Street; instead, it continues through town to the Ice Age Trail Alliance (IATA) headquarters. To complete the entire segment and add another mile to your total distance, follow the above route until the trail ends at Lewis Street and turn left (rather than right). Then turn right onto Caesar Street, following it to Main Street (US Highway 14) and watching for traffic as you cross Main. The Ice Age Trail Alliance (IATA) headquarters will be to your left. When you leave the IATA, cross Main Street again and turn left (west). In 0.25 mile, turn right (north) onto Hickory Street. From there, it's 0.3 mile back to your starting point.

39 Ice Age Trail: Table Bluff Segment

DISTANCE: 4.4 miles
ELEVATION GAIN: 560 feet
HIGH POINT: 1020 feet
DIFFICULTY: Moderate, with some challenging sections
FITNESS: Hikers
FAMILY FRIENDLY: Suitable for older children
DOG FRIENDLY: Leashed dogs only
AMENITIES: Parking lot, interpretative info
CONTACT/MAP: Ice Age Trail Alliance; map available online and on-site
GPS: N 43°8'37.5" W 89° 40'13.0"

GETTING THERE

Driving: From US Highway 12 in Middleton, take the US Highway 14/University Avenue exit and head west on Highway 14. Drive for 7.4 miles (through Cross Plains), then turn right onto County Road KP. Continue for 2.4 miles to Table Bluff Road. After 0.3 mile, the trailhead parking lot will be on the left.

A landscape of hills, rocky bluffs, and refreshing creeks is what draws so many outdoor enthusiasts to the Driftless region. The Table Bluff segment of the Ice Age Trail includes all three, and then some. The trail begins high on Table Bluff outside Cross Plains, and its gentle beginning through savannas of young oaks and rolling prairie belies the more rugged terrain ahead. On its 2.2-mile journey south, the Table Bluff trail passes through hardwood forests, crosses a creek, and traverses a wooded ridge to reach the route's highlight: an overlook above the Black Earth Creek watershed. A mix of level prairie trails and some steeper climbs, this hike is easy enough for a novice but also interesting enough for a more seasoned hiker. This route can also be hiked in reverse; there's a parking lot and trailhead at its southern end too.

GET MOVING

Begin a 4.4-mile out-and-back hike at the trailhead on Table Bluff Road. Follow the trail as it heads south from the parking lot through a small savanna. The young oaks here, with the same gnarled branches and jagged bark of older trees, look a bit like bonsai versions of their older siblings. At 0.2 mile, the trail splits. For now, veer left to follow the Ice Age Trail; you'll follow the white-blazed trail on your return trip. The trail heads up a ridge through prairie before turning west and switchbacking through woods.

At 0.7 mile, you'll reach another prairie and level ground. This restored area—a labor of love for volunteers—is full of native wildflowers in the summer, like shooting star, prairie smoke, and coneflowers. At the western end of the prairie, stay straight when another trail enters from the right. After this point, the trail again climbs into an oak and hickory forest, following a ridge for nearly a mile. At the 1.5-mile mark, the trail splits. Veer right to stay on the Ice Age Trail.

The trees will thin as you reach the 1.8-mile mark and near the overlook. You'll also spot a picnic shelter on the bluff. Take in the view of the Black Earth Creek valley below you; the smaller creek running in from the east is one of its many tributaries. Some hikers use this overlook as their turnaround point, but I think it's worth hiking down the south side of the bluff to complete the segment. The trail switchbacks through prairie (it was freshly burned on one of my recent trips) to the parking lot below. Just east of the parking lot are wetlands where you can sometimes see waterfowl (particularly during migration) and muskrats.

From the south parking lot trailhead, head up the bluff again. Back at the overlook, near the 2-mile mark, angle northwest toward the picnic shelter, then head north

The Table Bluff segment of the Ice Age Trail begins in a savanna of young oaks.

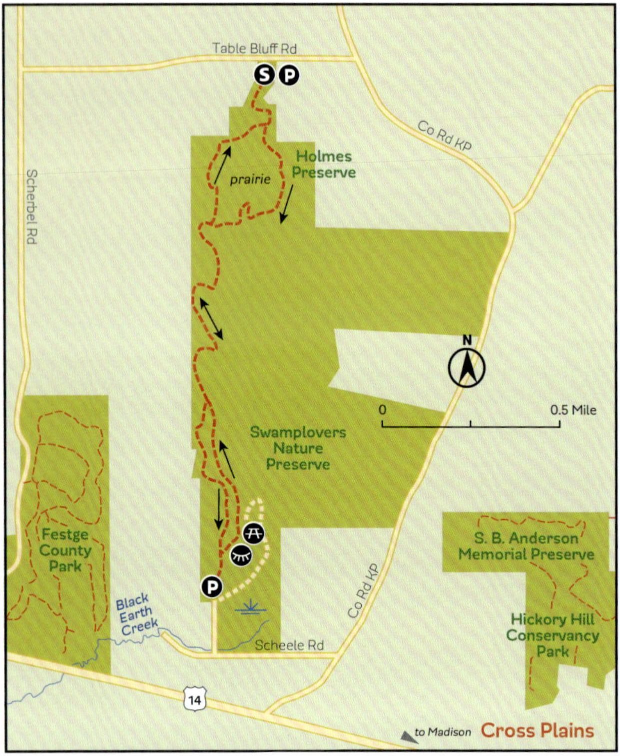

toward the woods. Follow the trail on the right, marked by white blazes, as it departs from the access road and heads into the woods. This trail parallels the Ice Age Trail until they join again at the 3-mile mark. At that point, keep following the trail north as you retrace your route. When you return to the prairie at 3.7 miles, turn left (north) to follow the white-blazed trail. For the next quarter mile, you'll hike through woods before entering prairie again. Then it's a short hike up a hill to rejoin the Ice Age Trail at the 4.2-mile mark, and finally, a quarter-mile hike back across Table Bluff to your starting point.

MAKE IT SHORTER

For a shorter hike that still includes the overlook, begin at the south trailhead parking lot on Scheele Road. From here, hike a 1.5-mile out-and-back up the bluff and through the forest. Head north on the white-blazed trail until the trail junction at 0.7 mile, then return south on the Ice Age Trail.

40 Cross Plains State Park

DISTANCE: 3 miles
ELEVATION GAIN: 410 feet
HIGH POINT: 1110 feet
DIFFICULTY: Easy to moderate, with some challenging sections
FITNESS: Hikers
FAMILY FRIENDLY: Suitable for older children; there are several steep sections throughout the hike.
DOG FRIENDLY: Leashed dogs only
AMENITIES: Parking lot
CONTACT/MAP: Wisconsin Department of Natural Resources; map available online
GPS: N 43°4'56.1" W 89°36'33.1"
BEFORE YOU GO: Although this public land is a state park, no vehicle admission sticker or trail pass is required.

GETTING THERE

Driving: From the junction of US Highway 12 and US Highway 14 in Middleton, head west on Highway 14. After 3.6 miles, turn left (south) on Cleveland Road. Continue for 0.9 mile to Old Sauk Pass. Turn right (west) onto Old Sauk Pass, and the trailhead parking lot will be ahead on the left.

Cross Plains State Park still feels like a secret. Nearly every time I've mentioned hiking here, I'm met with an incredulous:

"Cross Plains *State Park*?" Maybe it's because people expect state parks to have campgrounds and crowds. This little park, a few miles outside Madison, has neither. What it does have is some unexpectedly rugged hiking trails that run along a 100-foot gorge and through forest and prairie. As part of the larger Glacial Passage Area, the state park is adjacent to public lands managed by the Ice Age Trail Alliance and National Park Service (among other agencies) and shares a trailhead with the more popular Ice Age Trail. On my most recent hike here, the parking lot was half-full, but we met hardly anyone on the state park trails—an indication that many hikers still head to the southern trails instead.

GET MOVING

From the trailhead parking lot, cross Old Sauk Pass and turn right onto the trail that enters the woods past the Cross Plains State Park sign. For the first quarter mile, the rocky trail climbs along the east side of Wilkie Gorge, a deep ravine that's shrouded by trees most of the way. If you want a better look at the gorge, follow a short spur trail to an overlook at the 0.1-mile mark. (There are no fences or guardrails, so watch your footing and stay away from the edge.)

After this detour, return to the main trail and keep right at the next fork. Here the trail begins a long descent through the woods. Turn right again at the 0.3-mile mark; the trail will start to switchback down the hill. You'll finally reach level ground around the half mile mark and walk through a grove of tall pines. Beyond that, at 0.6 mile, the trail passes near the bottom of Wilkie Gorge at its north end.

Just beyond this point, begin another long climb past rock outcroppings. This shaded section is a good place to see ferns, mosses, and lichens. Keep right as another trail branches left. The trail tops out at the 0.8-mile mark, entering a large prairie plateau edged in oak savanna. Stay right to continue hiking this loop in a counterclockwise direction.

Early summer prairie at Cross Plains State Park

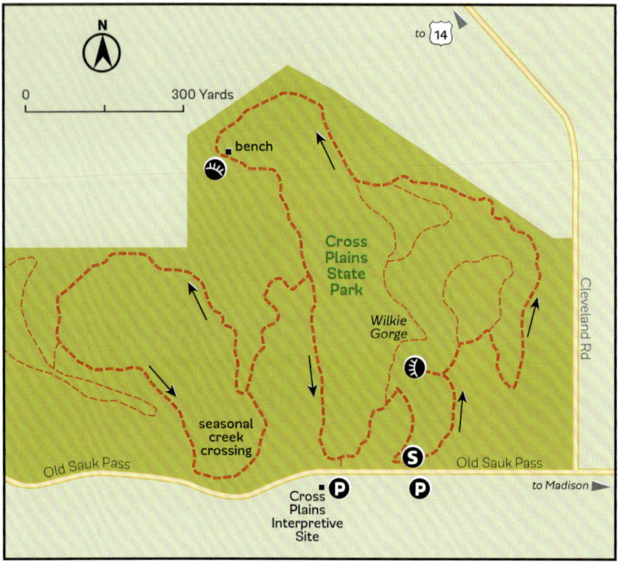

Along this section, there are some nice views through the oak savanna, including an overlook and bench at the 1-mile mark. The unusual turquoise water you see in the distance is Lake Katherine, an artificial lake belonging to a local quarry.

Turn right (west) at 1.2 miles when a trail heads deeper into the woods. This connector trail takes you to a newer trail section: a loop that twists and turns down a hillside, around a meadow, then up and along a wooded ridge. After a steep descent, the connector trail passes a bench at the 1.5-mile mark and enters the meadow. Turn right to follow the loop counterclockwise. Making a wide arc along the grassland's edge; the trail then heads up the opposite side of this small valley into the trees again. Stay left at 1.9 miles when another trail loop branches right. (Or take it if you'd like to add another 0.7 mile to your hike.) For the next quarter mile or so, the trail runs parallel along a ridge. In wet conditions, especially mud or snow, it can be slippery. There's a narrow but tricky seasonal creek to cross at 2.2 miles, with several large rocks to help you find your footing. After that, you'll soon return to the connector trail and retrace your route back up the hillside.

When you rejoin the main loop at 2.5 miles, turn right (south). Another prairie comes into view on your left as you continue toward Old Sauk Pass. When the trail turns east, there's a short connector trail south to the road if you're looking for a shortcut. Otherwise, follow the trail east and into the forest again—this time, it travels along the west side of Wilkie Gorge—for a short quarter-mile jaunt back to the starting point.

GO FARTHER

With a shared trailhead, it's easy to link the state park trails to other trails in the Glacial Passage Area, including the Ice Age Trail itself. After you finish the state park route, use the map at the trailhead to choose a trail on the south side of Old Sauk Pass.

GUIDE TO COMMON WILDFLOWERS

The Madison area isn't usually seen as a wildflower destination, but it should be. The first woodland wildflowers start sprouting as early as March and from then on, it's one wave of flower blooms after another until October. The best and brightest wildflower viewing is in our summer prairies and meadows—so if flowers are what you're hoping to see, time your hikes accordingly.

The following pages contain a visual guide for identifying common wildflowers that you may encounter on your hikes. Keep in mind that plant identification is easiest during a plant's bloom time.

1. Blazing star
2. Bloodroot
3. Bottle gentian
4. Celandine poppy
5. Chicory
6. Columbine
7. Common milkweed
8. Cup plant
9. Dutchman's Breeches
10. Field bindweed
11. Gray-headed coneflower
12. Large-flowered trillium

13. New England aster
14. Ox-eye daisy
15. Purple coneflower
16. Queen Anne's lace
17. Sweet Joe-pye weed
18. Turk's-cap lily
19. White snakeroot
20. White wild indigo
21. Wild bergamot
22. Wild geranium
23. Yellow jewelweed
24. Yellow trout lily

ACKNOWLEDGMENTS

Writing a book about hiking is not the same as simply hiking. This is a lesson I learned in the early stages of creating this book. As a new mom with a baby—then toddler—in tow, every hike I completed for my research was the result of teamwork. I'm grateful to all my hiking companions who were willing to lace up their boots and try a new trail with me: Dad, Mom, Gary, Jean, Lisa, Ivan, Gruffydd, and Gavin. More than anyone else, thank you, Peter, for joining me on so many hikes and for all the miles you carried our daughter on these trails. And thank you, Rose, for coming along for the ride and for making us smile.

Like the hikes themselves, writing this book required teamwork too, and I'm thankful to the team at Mountaineers Books for their expertise and encouragement. Thank you, Kate Rogers, Beth Jusino, and Callie Stoker-Graham for your editorial guidance and for making this book the best it could be. And thank you Ellis Failor-Rich for your design and layout work, and Bart Wright for your mapmaking.

And lastly, I want to express my gratitude to all the people, both past and present, who've stewarded the wild places and winding trails of the Madison area. Our community is a better place because of your restorative work.

An inlet at Warner Park leads to a lagoon and marsh (Trail 14).

RESOURCES

CONTACTS AND MAPS

Aldo Leopold Nature Center
(608) 221-0404
aldoleopoldnaturecenter.org

Blue Mound State Park
(608) 437-5711
dnr.wisconsin.gov/topic/parks/bluemound

City of Madison Parks Division
(608) 266-4711
cityofmadison.com/parks

Dane County Parks
(608) 224-3745
danecountyparks.com

Devil's Lake State Park
(608) 356-8301
dnr.wisconsin.gov/topic/parks/devilslake

Friends of Pope Farm Conservancy
popefarmconservancy.org

Governor Dodge State Park
(608) 935-2315
dnr.wisconsin.gov/topic/parks/govdodge

Ice Age Trail Alliance
(800) 227-0046
iceagetrail.org

Lake Kegonsa State Park
(608) 873-9695
dnr.wisconsin.gov/topic/parks/lakekegonsa

Lakeshore Nature Preserve
(608) 265-9275
lakeshorepreserve.wisc.edu

Madison Metropolitan School District
(608) 663-1879
madison.k12.wi.us

Monona East Side Business Alliance
(608) 416-1610
discovermonona.com

University of Wisconsin–Madison Arboretum
(608) 263-7888
arboretum.wisc.edu

Wisconsin Department of Natural Resources
(888) 936-7463
dnr.wisconsin.gov

LOCAL ORGANIZATIONS

Access Ability Wisconsin
(608) 886-9388
accessabilitywi.org

Dane County Humane Society's Wildlife Center
(608) 287-3235
giveshelter.org/wildlife-center

Dane County Parks Friends Groups
danecountyparks.com/Find-a-Friends-Group

Southern Wisconsin Bird Alliance
(608) 255-2473
swibirds.org

Wisconsin Master Naturalist Program
wimasternaturalist.org

INDEX

Wooded trail at Moraine Kettles Preserve (Trail 24)

S

T

U

V

W

Y

ABOUT THE AUTHOR

Andrea Debbink is a Madison-based naturalist and author who loves exploring the scenic beauty of the Midwest. Growing up in Minnesota, she hiked her first trails in the St. Croix River Valley and along the north shore of Lake Superior. Since then, her love of hiking has taken her to the top of Colorado's highest peaks, into the Utah desert, and on trails in England, Scotland, and Wales. When she's not hiking, Andrea writes nature-focused books for children and adults, including *If the Rivers Run Free*, *Flower Finding*, and the guided nature journal, *Thrive Where You're Planted*. She's also the creator of the *Natural Wonder* newsletter. Find out more about her work at andreadebbink.com.

OTHER TITLES YOU MIGHT ENJOY FROM MOUNTAINEERS BOOKS

Isle Royale National Park, 5th edition: Foot Trails and Water Routes

Jim DuFresne

The "backcountry bible" to one of Michigan's most beautiful national parks!

Campfire Stories: Tales from America's National Parks

Ilyssa and Dave Kyu, editors

Intimate, compelling, and share-out-loud tales about our national parks

Knowing the Trees: Discover the Forest from Seed to Snag

Ken Keffler

An engaging, fact-filled, and beautifully illustrated guide to a forest's life cycle

Birding for Boomers: And Everyone Else Brave Enough to Embrace the World's Most Rewarding and Frustrating Activity

Sneed Collard

A laugh-out-loud crash course on how to easily observe, understand, and enjoy birds–at any age!